FROM GLORY TO GLORY

Daily faith food for your spirit.

VOLUME 1.

Rita Ladejobi

FROM GLORY TO GLORY

FIRST EDITION, 2021

ISBN: 979-8-88525-668-1

Preface

Many Christians are busy with so many things. They are engaged with activities for the Lord. But they neglect the most important thing: spending time with God. They feed their bodies three meals a day and their spirit one meal a week. To be strong in faith, we need to feed our faith daily with the word of God. These bite-sized pieces of faith food will help you feed your faith daily as you study and meditate on the daily scriptures; Gods truth will register on your Spirit and empower you.

Content

January

February

Content

Content

May

June

Content

July

August

Content

September

October

Content

November

December

January 1

Genesis 1-2; Matthew 1

I will go before you

Isaiah 45:2
I will go before thee, and make the crooked places straight: I will break in pieces the gates of brass, and cut in sunder the bars of iron:

This promise is for you, child of God. God has gone ahead of you into this new year to remove all impediments and obstructions out of your way. He will help you to surmount all difficulties. God is faithful to fulfil all his promises. If you agree with Him in faith, He will open your spiritual eyes and show you hidden things you need to know as you fellowship with him daily. God will also break the gates of brass and cut the bars of iron asunder; this means that both spiritual and physical barriers erected to stop you from fulfilling your divine destiny will be shattered by God.

Confession: Thank you, Father. I believe You are going before me into this new year to perfect all that concerns me.

January 2

Genesis 3-5; Matthew 2

The secret place

Psalm 91:14
Because he hath set his love upon me, therefore will I deliver him: I will set him on high, because he hath known my name.

Reading through the book of Psalm 91, you will notice that it is full of God's promised blessings for those who dwell in his presence continually. The secret place of God is his presence. The actual test of your love for him is how much time you spend with him in fellowship and the study of his word. How much time you give to his service. How much love you show to people around you and your willingness to obey his word in all things. The above scripture says, "because he has set his love upon me," which is the key to all the blessings in Psalm 91. Your love for God will cause you to spend time with him just as people in love will spend quality time together.

Confession: Father, I receive grace to do what Your word says because I love You.

January 3

Genesis 6-8; Matthew 3

Gratitude

Psalm 95:10
Forty years long was I grieved with this generation, and said, It is a people that do err in their heart, and they have not known my ways

God was angry with his children because of their wrong attitude; their heart was not right. They were not grateful for the past victories he gave them. They did not acknowledge his provisions, protection, and divine intervention in their journey. Their attitude really displeased the Lord. Remember, his ways are not our ways. God has a better plan than what you are thinking. When we are grateful for what he has done, he will be pleased to do more. We can look beyond the problem at hand and appreciate him for who he is. Your past victory is fuel to your faith.

Confession: Lord, I will give You thanks in all things, even when I don't understand.

January 4

Genesis 9-11; Matthew 4

Do you know His Name

Daniel 3:17
If it be so, our God whom we serve is able to deliver us from the burning fiery furnace, and he will deliver us out of thine hand, O king.

Your acknowledgement of who God is in any situation will strengthen your faith to keep you standing firm during challenges. The three Hebrew children knew God as their deliverer, so they answered the king, "If it is so, our God whom we serve is able to deliver us from the burning fiery furnace, and he will deliver us out of thine hand, O king." Abraham knew him as the great provider. He stepped out in faith to sacrifice his only son Isaac. But God stopped him and provided a ram for the sacrifice. Do you know his name in your present situation?

Confession: Lord, I believe that You are my deliverer in all situations.

January 5

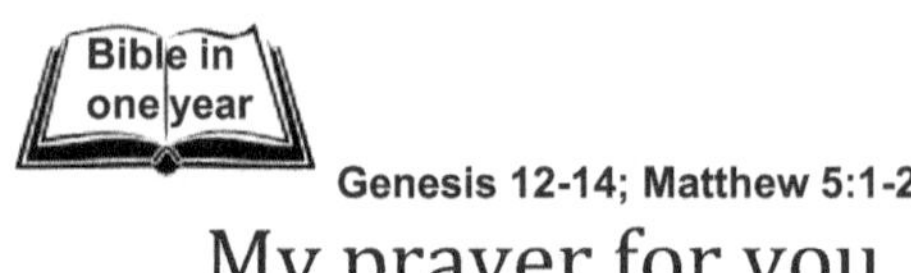

Genesis 12-14; Matthew 5:1-2

My prayer for you

Philippians 1:9
And this I pray, that your love may abound yet more and more in knowledge and all judgment

You are where you are today because of what you know. My prayer for you in this new year is that you will live a life of sincere love so Jesus will be proud of you and that you will increase in knowledge and practical insight. You will know what to do when you have an understanding of your present situation. "Knowledge is power, but liberty comes through wisdom." The book of proverbs 9:10 says, "The fear of the LORD *is* the beginning of wisdom, and the knowledge of the Holy One *is* understanding". So you can start by rededicating your life to God and determine to live a life of obedience to his word.

Confession: Lord, help me to grow more and more in love and practical insight.

January 6

Genesis 15-17; Matthew 5:27-48

Watered garden

Isaiah 58:11

And the Lord shall guide thee continually, and satisfy thy soul in drought, and make fat thy bones: and thou shalt be like a watered garden, and like a spring of water, whose waters fail not.

The image of a well-watered garden paints the picture of people whose God continually sustains. People who are fruitful and productive. God desires to sustain His chosen people, both physically and spiritually, as a testimony of hope to the world. A testimony that points people to our loving and faithful Father. The same is promised to each one of us, his children! he is our guide; he will satisfy our needs and strengthen us as we trust in him.

Confession: Lord, I trust you to guide me continually and satisfy my soul. I shall be like a watered garden.

January 7

Genesis 18-19; Matthew 6

Keep moving

Joshua 1:9
Have not I commanded thee? Be strong and of a good courage; be not afraid, neither be thou dismayed: for the Lord thy God is with thee whithersoever thou goest.

The scripture above commands us as Christians to be strong and courageous, which means developing the capacity to meet dangers and difficulties with firmness. When you are bold, you will move on in life no matter what happens. So keep moving, keep believing, don't allow yourself to be stagnant. Go through another door if one is not responding. Rise up like a brave soldier and move on. If you have missed your way, go back to where you started and retrace your steps.

Confession: I am strong and courageous. I will keep moving no matter what may come my way.

January 8

Genesis 20-22; Matthew 7

As we behold Him

2 Corinthians 3:18
But we all, with open face beholding as in a glass the glory of the Lord, are changed into the same image from glory to glory, even as by the Spirit of the Lord.

There is a transformation going on in you right now as you are taking time to study the word of God. You are beholding his glory, and in it lies all you need in life: instruction, conviction, correction, restoration, and training in righteousness. As you study the word of God, you are learning to live in conformity to God's will. You have to memorize and meditate on the instruction or corrections you receive from the word of God every day and practice them.

Confession: I will be transformed as I study the word of God; I will give more time to behold His glory every day.

January 9

Genesis 23-24; Matthew 8

The Spirit of power

2 Timothy 1:7
For God hath not given us the spirit of fear; but of power, and of love, and of a sound mind.

You already have the spirit of power, love, and a sound mind. The Spirit of power is the Holy Ghost living inside of you. As a believer, you have the power of God residing in you. You can dominate any situation or circumstances that confront you. You can decree and declare what you want. You have the power over sicknesses and diseases. You cannot enjoy what you have if you are not aware of it. You can declare the above scripture over yourself daily, enforcing the reality of the power of God within you. Fear opens the door for the enemy to attack, so when anxiety shows up, be quick to exercise power within you and decree, "you spirit of fear, I resist you get, out in Jesus' name."

Confession: I have the spirit of power, love, and a sound mind. I am not afraid. God is for me.

January 10

Genesis 25-26; Matthew 9:1-17

Focus on Christ, not on crisis

Hebrews 12:2
Looking unto Jesus the author and finisher of our faith; who for the joy that was set before him endured the cross, despising the shame, and is set down at the right hand of the throne of God.

To look unto Jesus means to give him undivided attention, purposefully looking away and putting off everything else that will serve as a distraction. One of the ways you can achieve this is by focusing on his promises until you see the physical manifestation of your desires. I shared the practical ways you can do this in my book "Just one word from God." If I am dealing with any issue, I will write out scriptures concerning that issue and prophesy them day and night. In the place of confession and meditation, the light will come, and darkness will flee when the light comes.

Confession: I will focus on His promises until I see the physical manifestation of all my desires.

January 11

Genesis 27-28; Matthew 9:18-38

Great reward

Hebrews 10:35
Cast not away therefore your confidence, which hath great recompence of reward.

What are your dreams, what are you trusting God for? What is your heart desires? It would be best to keep them alive by working on them daily, writing them down, and placing them in a strategic place where you can see them every day. Then you can create a strategic plan to achieve your dream. It's essential that you take one day at a time and be focused. Don't allow yourself to be distracted by friends or the things happening around you. Remember, your confidence in the Lord will be greatly rewarded. Your trust in his saving grace and divine intervention will keep you above the storm.

Confession: I refuse to be distracted. I am focused, I believe that I will be greatly rewarded as I trust in the Lord.

January 12

Genesis 29-30; Matthew 10:1-23

Assurance

John 6:69
And we believe and are sure that thou art that Christ, the son of the living God.

Peter says that by personal revelation and experience, they have come to know that Jesus is Christ, the son of the living God. You need an intimate revelation of God to stand and testify like Job "For I know that my redeemer lives." Trials and temptations will come, but you will go after other gods if you don't know him yet. Jesus asked the twelve disciples in John 6:67, "Will ye also go away? Peter replied, "Lord to whom we shall go? You have the words of eternal life"; you have the key to abundant life. There is no help from anywhere else. Some of our life experiences have a way of bringing us to a deeper relationship with God; we need to get to that place where we can say, "I know him, whom I have believed."

Confession: Lord, I want to know You more; take me deeper in You.

January 13

Genesis 31-32; Matthew 10:24-42

The good fight

1 Timothy 6:12
Fight the good fight of faith, lay hold on eternal life, whereunto thou art also called, and hast professed a good profession before many witnesses.

Good fight? Yes, the battle of faith is a good fight; we need to take possession of the good things God has freely given to us, good health, joy, and peace in all areas of our lives. Abundant life is yours, but there is an armed robber whose mission is to kill, steal and destroy. He comes with tricks to discourage you, sad and bitter thoughts towards people who might have mistreated you. He aims to steal all that belongs to you and prevent you from moving forward in life. It would be best to fight against unforgiveness so that you can move on in life. Your weapon is the word of God. You can remind the devil what God said in His word concerning you.

Confession: I will fight the good fight of faith and take back all that the devil has stolen from me.

January 14

Genesis 33-35; Matthew 11

How to overcome

1 John 5:4
For whatsoever is born of God overcometh the world: and this is the victory that overcometh the world, even our faith.

The Lord Jesus Christ is the only man who has ever confronted and defeated the devil, thereby becoming the only one to ever truly and ultimately overcome the world. Jesus clearly announced, "I have overcome the world." (John 16:33). Anyone who puts his faith in the person of Jesus Christ and His finished redemptive work becomes a partaker in Christ's victory over the world and its lusts. The believer who overcomes the world is the one who still maintains his focus, allegiance, loyalty, dedication, or commitment to Jesus Christ and His cause, despite the abounding distractions, temptations, tribulations, or persecutions he faces or encounters in the world (Heb. 6:10-12).

Confession: I am victorious. Glory be to God who has given us victory.

January 15

Genesis 36-37; Matthew 12:1-21

I have prayed for you

Luke 22:32
But I have prayed for thee, that thy faith fail not: and when thou art converted, strengthen thy brethren.

Your faith in God is so precious that the devil will do so much to get you off your faith in the Lord Jesus. The temptations and challenging situations make us doubt God's love for us. We all have denied him at one time or the other. We reject him when we fail to do the word of God because of fear of the unknown, fear of what people will say. We are so worried about tomorrow when the word of God says, "do not worry." Jesus is saying to you the same word he said to peter "I have prayed for you that in it all, your faith which is more precious than gold will not fail."

Confession: I have confidence in You, Lord. Help me not deny You in any situation.

January 16

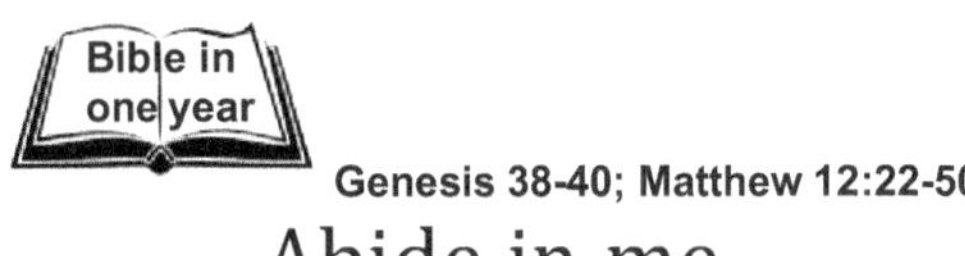

Genesis 38-40; Matthew 12:22-50

Abide in me

John 15:7
If ye abide in me, and my words abide in you, ye shall ask what ye will, and it shall be done unto you.

The scripture above is one of the secrets to answered prayer. The word of God must abide in you because the devil cannot defeat a child of God full of the word of God. When you memorize and meditate on the word of God, the Holy Spirit gives you a complete understanding of the words of God. This will positively affect your thinking, mindset, will, and desire. His choice will become your will. And God will grant your wishes because they are according to his will for your life. When the word of God abides in us, when we are rooted and grounded in the word, we will produce fruits of righteousness, faith and holiness.

Confession: I will memorize and meditate on the word of God daily so that I can bear more fruit to advance the kingdom of God.

January 17

Genesis 41; Matthew 13:1-32

Resist the devil

James 4:7
Submit yourselves therefore to God. Resist the devil, and he will flee from you.

Before you can resist the devil, you need to submit to God, his ways, counsel, and precept. You need to be a doer of the word. You cannot live in disobedience and exercise authority over Satan. You need healing in your body, yet you refuse to obey the word of God that says you should forgive. God has given us the power to resist the devil's plan over our lives, children, business etc.. But we constantly open the door for him by not walking in obedience to the ways of God. Without submission, you have no authority. Your compliance must be complete, then you can resist the devil, and he will flee from you just like Jesus did in Luke 4:3-13.

Confession: Lord, I receive grace to submit to You in all things.

January 18

Genesis 42-43; Matthew 13:33-58

Abundant life

John 10:10
The thief cometh not, but for to steal, and to kill, and to destroy: I am come that they might have life and that they might have it more abundantly.

Abundant life does not come from material possessions, houses, cars, and money. That is why you see many wealthy people, yet they are not happy. Abundant life is eternal life, a life that begins the moment we come to Christ and receive Him as Savior, and it goes on throughout all eternity. It's a life of righteousness, peace, and joy; it's a life where the situation and circumstances of life do not determine your happiness. The secret to enjoying this abundant life in Christ is found in John 15:7. We are admonished to abide in him and let his word abide in us continually.

Confession: I have abundant life in Christ Jesus, a life of righteousness, peace, and joy.

January 19

Genesis 44-45; Matthew 14:1-21

The gate is open

Hebrews 7:19
For the law made nothing perfect, but the bringing in of a better hope did; by the which we draw nigh unto God.

Yes, the gate is open because we have Jesus, our high priest, who lives forever interceding for all the saints. The former priest could not continue in their office because they were subject to death. But Jesus Christ has acquired for us a better ministry. Having this confidence, we can come boldly to the throne of grace knowing that we have a better covenant with excellent promises. Don't allow the devil to hold you down with guilt. Therefore, if the Son shall make you free, ye shall be free indeed (John 8:36). You can come boldly to the throne of grace.

Confession: Thank You, Jesus, for interceding for me. I am free indeed.

January 20

Genesis 46-48; Matthew 14:22-36

You are righteous

2 Corinthians 5:21
For He made Him who knew no sin to be sin for us, that we might become the righteousness of God in Him.

Our self-acclaimed righteousness did not merit us a right standing before God. Our holiness, works, prayers, devotion, church activities, fellowship with the brethren, and fasting does not make us receive his righteousness. We only received God's righteousness because of the love, kindness, mercy, and grace of Jesus Christ, our Savior. Jesus took it upon himself to endure the cross. Though blameless, he willingly gave his life for us. We need to maintain a lifestyle that portrays holiness, devotion, obedience, peace, trust, and love of God in words and deeds. It is an acceptance of our heritage as children of God, enabling us to come boldly before our Heavenly Father despite our inadequacies and flaws as human beings.

Confession: Thank you, Lord, for the gift of righteousness.

January 21

Genesis 49-50; Matthew 15:1-20

Grieve not the Holy Spirit

Ephesians 4:30-31
And grieve not the holy Spirit of God, whereby ye are sealed unto the day of redemption. Let all bitterness, and wrath, and anger, and clamour, and evil speaking, be put away from you, with all malice:

How can we grieve the holy Spirit? By allowing bitterness, anger, evil speaking, and malice. The holy Spirit is grieved when we cannot control our emotions. The Bible says that anger rests in the bosom of fools. (Ecclesiastes 7:9). The Holy Spirit can be grieved by what we do, what we think, and what goes on in our hearts. Let us guide against speaking evil of one another or being revengeful. Remember, he is our comforter; He is willing to heal our hearts if we allow Him.

Confession: Lord help me not to grieve the Holy Spirit; I will walk in love towards people.

January 22

Exodus 1-3; Matthew 15:21-39

They are common to man

1 Corinthians 10:13
There hath no temptation taken you but such as is common to man: but God is faithful, who will not suffer you to be tempted above that ye are able; but will with the temptation also make a way to escape, that ye may be able to bear it.

"But such as is common to man" This means that what you are going through or will ever go through in life, someone has gone through it. They are common to human experience. Your approach to the situation determines your victory over that problem. You need to be free from anxiety and worry. Let the peace of God rest in your heart. Don't try to do what only God can do. The scripture above says that God will make a way of escape. Remember, He makes a way where there is no way. Do your part by standing in faith and blessing others, just like Joseph did while in prison.

Confession: Lord Jesus, I confess that You are faithful. I believe that You will make way for me.

January 23

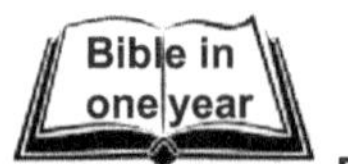

Exodus 4-6; Matthew 16

Before I was afflicted

Psalm 119:67
"Before I was afflicted I went astray: but now have I kept thy word."

The psalmist admitted that he went his own way before his troubles came, doing whatever he wanted. His life was in his own hands until affliction came, and then he realized that he had been in charge of his life. But now, he has decided to keep the word of God. To give God first place in his life and walk in obedience to God's ways. Sometimes God will do whatever it takes to get our attention. One of the purposes of affliction is to teach us things we would not otherwise know. Until hard times come, our knowledge of God and His Word tends to be theoretical. But we don't have to wait for trouble before we keep His word.

Confession: Lord, I will give You first place in my life, Holy Spirit; I receive Your guidance.

January 24

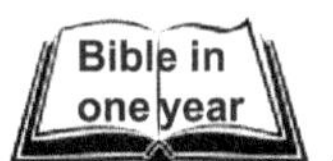

Exodus 7-8; Matthew 17

I live for Christ

Philippians 1:21
For to me to live is Christ, and to die is gain.

Apostle Paul is saying here that from the time of his conversion until his martyrdom, every move he made aimed at advancing the gospel and the Church of Christ. Paul's singular aim was to bring glory to Jesus. This should be our aimas believers., To live is Christ means that Christ is our focus, goal, and chief desire. Christ is the centre of our mind, heart, body, and soul. Everything that we do, we do for Christ's glory. As we run the "race marked out for us," we lay aside the entangling sin and worldly distractions, "fixing our eyes on Jesus" (Hebrews 12:1-2).

Confession: For me to live is Christ. Everything I do will be for His glory.

January 25

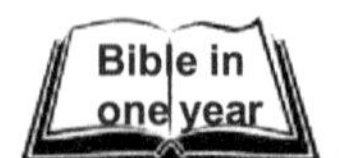

Exodus 9-10; Matthew 18:1-20

Humility

1 Peter 5:5
Likewise, ye younger, submit yourselves unto the elder. Yea, all of you be subject one to another, and be clothed with humility: for God resisteth the proud, and giveth grace to the humble.

The scripture above says that God resists the proud but gives grace to the humble. This means that humility is the virtue that qualifies you for more grace. Humility is often characterized by genuine gratitude and lack of arrogance, a modest view of self. But we are not born with humility; it is cultivated. One of the ways you can develop a spirit of humility is by focusing on Jesus and becoming more like him.Another way is to start serving others and giveahelping hand to hurting people even when you are hurting too. Jesus said I am among you as one who serves. Luke 22:27.

Confession: Lord, I receive grace to cultivate the spirit of humility by focusing on God and helping people around me.

January 26

Exodus 11-12; Matthew 18:21-35

The persistent enemy

Genesis 39:10
And it came to pass, as she spake to Joseph day by day, that he hearkened not unto her, to lie by her, or to be with her.

Persistence is one of the weapons the enemy uses to get a result. The scripture above says that she spoke to Joseph daily to lie with her. But because he did not yield to her suggestion. She decided to lie against Joseph. Though Joseph went to prison, God was with him. He was later promoted from prison to prime minister. God has a glorious future for all his children, but the enemy will always come through different ways to steal, kill, and destroy. The enemy was just after his glorious destiny. Thank God that he overcame. What do you think would have happened to Joseph if he had complied with the temptation? The grace of God is available to help us to be focused and refuse to yield to temptations because there is a glorious future ahead.

Confession: Lord help me not to yield to temptation; I receive grace to be focused.

January 27

Exodus 13-15; Matthew 19:1-15

Men ought always to pray

Luke 18:1
And he spake a parable unto them to this end, that men ought always to pray, and not to faint

God hears and answers our prayers. But he does not speak much. Just one word from God can give you a supernatural turnaround. The unjust judge answered the widow because she did not give up; she kept coming to the judge until her request was granted. How much more will God answer those who seek Him diligently. (Luke 18:1-8). Prayer is not only when you kneel. It is continual communication with God. You can communicate with your heavenly Father while driving, cooking, or walking. I find praying in tongues very helpful as I go about my daily activities. It helps me to be conscious of His indwelling presence.

Confession: I will not faint. I will trust Him until I see the physical manifestation of my prayers.

January 28

Exodus 16-18; Matthew 19:16-30

The yoke shall be destroyed

Isaiah 10:27
It shall come to pass in that day That his burden will be taken away from your shoulder, And his yoke from your neck, And the yoke will be destroyed because of the anointing oil.

The anointing of God upon your life will destroy the yoke of any problem that is confronting you and your family. God's yoke destroying power can set you free. But you need to activate the residual anointing of God in you through a deeper relationship with God in prayer and the study of his word and reading spiritual books. There are dimensions of God's anointing. The deeper you go with him, the more his anointing will increase in your life. There is room for an increase for those willing to pay the price and go deeper in God. Are you ready to go deeper in God?

Confession: Lord, take me deeper in You. Let there be an increase of Your anointing upon my life.

January 29

Exodus 19-21; Matthew 20:1-16

I will have mercy

Romans 9:15
For he saith to Moses, I will have mercy on whom I will have mercy, and I will have compassion on whom I will have compassion.

Demonstrating mercy is one way God reveals His glory." When God said, "I will have mercy on whom I will have mercy," he meant that he would show kindness, compassion, and forgiveness to anyone He chooses. God does not show mercy because humans deserve it. God's mercy cannot be earned by status, social class, or works of righteousness. It is a blessing to know that covenant mercies are God's exclusive property to bestow upon whom He will. “Unto Thee, O LORD, belongeth mercy.” (Ps. 62:12) “To the Lord our God belong mercies and forgivenesses, though we have rebelled against Him.” (Dan. 9:9) He is “the Father of mercies,” and it is His sovereign right to confer them upon, or withhold them from, whom He will.

Confession: Lord, behold the blood of Jesus Christ and show me your mercy.

January 30

Exodus 22-24; Matthew 20:17-34

Time of favor

Psalm 102:13
Thou shalt arise, and have mercy upon Zion: for the time to favour her, yea, the set time, is come.

Yes, the set time has come. There is a set time for the favour of God to manifest in your life. Divine favour is an uncommon blessing or breakthrough that God Himself has orchestrated and ordained for your life. It positions you for success and transcends all barriers. They may be racial, social, cultural, financial, relational, or even generational. God compasses us roundabout with His favour because of our righteousness, which we received from Jesus Christ. Divine favour of God does not come to your life because of what you have done. But because you have confessed Jesus as your Lord and Saviour. Your part is to respond to Him by creating an atmosphere of worship and devotion to God. Not only will you attract His presence, but you will keep heaven open over your life and his divine favour flowing towards you.

Confession: This is my time of divine visitation. I will create an atmosphere for His divine visitation.

January 31

Exodus 25-26; Matthew 21:1-22

Path of life

Psalm 16:11
Thou wilt shew me the path of life: in thy presence is fullness of joy; at thy right hand there are pleasures for evermore.

God has a path for each one of his children to follow. When we discover and follow his ways, it will attract his presence, and pleasures always lie in it. God is committed to showing those who are willing to trust him the path of life. Those that have made God their source will not lack the oil of joy. The way of life is what God makes known to us, not as a trail to follow but as a promise to embrace. When you read the whole chapter of Psalm 16, you will notice the glorious shift in it. It begins with our faith in God and ends with God's faithfulness to us. He will not abandon us. No, he won't. He makes known to us the path of life, even life beyond the grave.

Confession*:* "Lord, I'm so grateful that You will show me where the path is and travel with me on my journey."

February 1

Exodus 27-28; Matthew 21:23-46

God will fight for you

Deuteronomy 1:30
The Lord your God, who goes before you, He will fight for you, according to all He did for you in Egypt before your eyes.

We all fight battles, but the actual battlefield is your mind. If you can win the battle in your mind, you can win every other struggle: emotional, financial, health, or the battle against your marriage and children. We face battles every day. For every battle you face, including the one you are fighting right now, God says, "Do not be terrified, or afraid of the problems that are confronting you right now. Because the Lord your God goes before you, he will fight for you." Put your God before your fears and fight the battles on your knees in prayer. A victorious mind will believe this word of God and declare it every day.

Confession: Lord, I believe that You are going before me to fight all my battles.

February 2

Exodus 29-30; Matthew 22:1-22

They overcame

Revelation 12:11
And they overcame him by the blood of the Lamb and by the word of their testimony, and they did not love their lives to the death.

The scripture gives us vivid pictures of Christ's redemptive work on the cross. Peter explains that "God paid a ransom" to save us from our old empty way of life. The ransom was not paid with mere gold or silver, which will lose its value. It was the precious blood of Christ. (1 Peter 1:18–19) . You can overcome that addiction and that sinful habit because Christ has given you victory through his blood and the word of your testimony. Man believes with the heart, and with the mouth, confession is made unto salvation. It is the same process. You need to play your part by declaring your victory in Christ daily. You can get my book on amazon, "Just one word from God" you will find It helpful in your daily declaration of your victory in Christ.

Confession: Thank You, Father, for making me an overcomer.

February 3

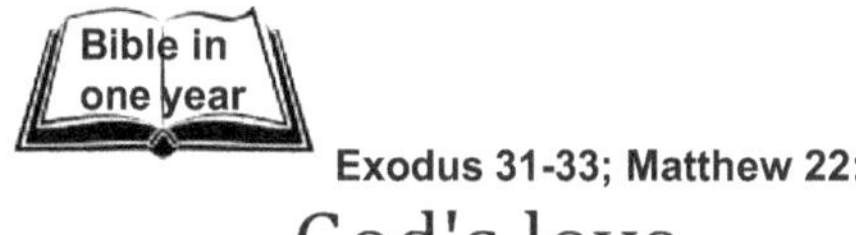

Exodus 31-33; Matthew 22:23-46

God's love

1 Corinthians 13:13
And now abide faith, hope, love, these three; but the greatest of these is love.

Why is love the greatest? Because God is love" (1 John 4:7-8). God created us out of His love, and that love is from God alone. The love of God is the greatest. Faith, hope, and love always go together. In John 13:34–35, Jesus says, "A new command I give you: Love one another, as I have loved you, so you must love one another. By this, everyone will know that you are my disciples if you love one another." Love always requires another as an object; love cannot remain within itself, and that is part of what makes love the greatest gift. The Bible says that the love of God is shed abroad in our hearts (Romance 5:5-11); we need to practice the love of God in our hearts consciously.

Confession: Thank You, Lord, for Your love; I receive grace to walk in love.

February 4

Exodus 34-36; Matthew 23:1-22

Let your hearts be established

James 5:8
Be ye also patient; stablish your hearts: for the coming of the Lord draweth nigh.

The word "establish" means *to make fast, to confirm.* A Christian cannot move forward in the Christian life without a firm faith. The basis of our stability as Christians is our faith in Christ. The troubles are only temporary. God has a plan, and He will execute that plan right on time and in His perfect way. There is no place for double-minded, unstable believers. They are like the wave of the sea driven and tossed by the wind. The scripture above admonishes us to be patient. We are to develop an attitude of longsuffering and trust in God. We should not overly concern ourselves about the things in this world but be prepared for the imminent return of Christ. We are to live with the consciousness that his coming could be at any moment.

Confession: I will wait patiently for the Lord; I refuse to be moved by circumstances.

February 5

Exodus 37-38; Matthew 23:23-39

Declare the works of the Lord

Psalm 118:17
I shall not die, but live, And declare the works of the Lord.

This is a proclamation of faith by the psalmist! He declares that he will not die but live to declare the works of the LORD. The psalmist dealt with circumstances and situations that threatened his very existence. His conditions might not be the same as ours, but many of us face challenges of varying severity today. Like the Psalmist, we can declare in the same spirit of faith, "I shall not die, but live, and declare the works of the LORD." This is not positive thinking or having an optimistic worldview. It is putting our trust and faith in God, who can rescue us from everything that is threatening our life. When He brings you through that situation, you will live to tell the story. You will live to declare the works of the LORD in your generation and those to come.

Confession: I shall not die, but live, and declare the works of the Lord.

February 6

Exodus 39-40; Matthew 24:1-22

Appointed time

Habakkuk 2:3
For the vision is yet for an appointed time; But at the end it will speak, and it will not lie. Though it tarries, wait for it; Because it will surely come, It will not tarry.

I have discovered that when you think God is not doing anything, that's when he is doing the most. He is putting all the pieces together, lining things up, setting up a divine appointment, and preparing us for the assignment he has for us. Wow, it is not easy to wait, is it? We want it now. The scripture says that there is an appointed time for that vision to come to pass, so wait for it. It will surely come. God is faithful to carry out His plans and purposes at his appointed time and to finish the good work he began in us while we are waiting, take time to develop yourself spiritually, and let the peace of God flood your heart.

Confession: Lord, I receive grace to wait for Your appointed time.

February 7

Leviticus 1-3; Matthew 24:23-51

How to dress up

Colossians 3:12
Therefore, as the elect of God, holy and beloved, put on tender mercies, kindness, humility, meekness, longsuffering

We are instructed to clothe ourselves with these qualities mentioned above. So when we arise in the morning, as we put on socks, shorts, shirts, and skirts, We are to clothe ourselves also with the fruits of the Spirit. Socks and shorts are pretty easy to put on each morning. What about compassion, kindness, gentleness, humility, patience, forgiveness, and love? So how does it work? How can these positive virtues be seen in our lives? Doing what the Bible commands here is not possible with the fleshly nature. Humanity, in general, is going in the opposite direction with so much conflict, selfishness, pride, and ungratefulness. But we have the spirit of God dwelling in us as Christians. Our mission is to allow him to work in us and through us.

Confession: Lord, I receive grace to allow the fruits of the Holy Spirit in me to manifest.

February 8

Leviticus 4-6; Matthew 25:1-30

By the grace of God

1 Corinthians 15:10
But by the grace of God I am what I am, and His grace toward me was not in vain; but I labored more abundantly than they all, yet not I, but the grace of God which was with me.

Apostle Paul recognized that everything he went through prepared him to fulfil his purpose by the grace of God. So rather than focussing on the fact that he was different from others, Paul continued by saying, "But by the grace of God I am what I am." Though he had no earthly experience with Jesus as the other apostles did, he was mightily anointed and perfectly gifted and fitted for the call God had given him to reach the Gentile world. Don't allow the devil to torment you by telling you that something is wrong because you are not like others. Your differences make you unique. God gave you specific characteristics and personality traits because you need them for the assignment He has planned for your life.

Confession: Thank You, Father; I am what I am, by the grace of God.

February 9

Leviticus 7-9; Matthew 25:31-46

Awake out of sleep

Romans 13:11
And do this, knowing the time, that now it is high time to awake out of sleep; for now our salvation is nearer than when we first believed.

Wake up! Arise, Christian. It is time to awaken from sleep. We are called to wake from any spiritual slumber, "for now our salvation draws ever closer." Christ is coming to take us to be with Himself, and the time is getting nearer. Those in the early Church were encouraged to get ready for the return of the Lord Jesus. And two thousand years later, this instruction still stands. But it's very urgent. Every day that passes is one day closer to when the trumpet will sound. The dead in Christ will rise from their graves in incorruptible bodies. And we who are alive and remain will be caught up, together with them, into the cloud to meet JESUS in the air. Let us become alert and ready, watching and waiting for his soon return. And let us seek to use the time we have left on earth.

Confession: Lord, help me to wake up from any spiritual slumber.

February 10

Leviticus 10-12; Matthew 26:1-19

The blessed man

Jeremiah 17:7
Blessed is the man that trusteth in the LORD, and whose hope the LORD is.

Trusting in the Lord is simply believing what God has said. It is having faith in the incarnate word of God and trusting all that the Lord has revealed to us through the written word of God, or rhema, which is the spoken word of God. The man who trusts in the Lord simply believes him in all things, believes his word, trusts his promises and does not allow himself to be shaken by circumstances, sight, emotions, or feelings. Blessed indeed is the man that trusts in the Lord. Favoured and fortunate is the one whose hope is resting in the God of our salvation. You may not look like it now, but you are loaded with his blessings and highly favoured. You are blessed to bless others.

Confession: I am blessed because I trust and hope in the Lord.

February 11

Leviticus 13; Matthew 26:20-54

Acknowledge him

Proverbs 3:5-6
Trust in the Lord with all your heart, And lean not on your own understanding; In all your ways acknowledge Him, And He shall direct your paths.

"Trust in the Lord with all your heart" means placing our heart at the Lord's feet. This surrender leaves no room for anxiety or worry. But wholly entrusts our "self" to God's sovereignty. "Lean not on your own understanding" is to lean wholly into the strong arms of God. "In all your ways acknowledge Him," It means that we recognize he is God, and we acknowledge his authority in what we are doing, even in our daily activities. I always ask for His help and wisdom while cooking, even though I am a professional cook. I do not depend on what I know but on God. "And He will direct your paths" this means that he will begin to establish our steps and lead us where he needs us.

Confession: Lord, I receive grace to acknowledge You in all my ways.

February 12

Leviticus 14; Matthew 26:55-75

What are you saying

Numbers 14:28
Say unto them, As truly as I live, saith the Lord, as ye have spoken in mine ears, so will I do to you.

Many of us do not realize that there is life in our words. If we want to start seeing the promise of God manifest in our lives, we will have to speak words of faith. The Israelites murmured words of unbelief. Little did they realize that God would take them at their word. God will do what you say concerning your present situation, home, children, visions, and dreams. The angels are standing by to hearken to your words, so spend time speaking out what you want to see every day. You need to water your seed in prayer by speaking what God says concerning the issue.

Confession: Lord, help me speak what Your word says in every situation.

February 13

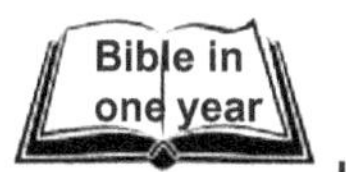

Leviticus 15-17; Matthew 27:1-31

You will hear a word

Isaiah 30:21
Your ears shall hear a word behind you, saying, "This is the way, walk in it," Whenever you turn to the right hand Or whenever you turn to the left.

Like Israel, we nurture our brand of foolishness and lock ourselves into alternative cycles of resistance. Sometimes we just want to do things our way and in our strength. But God's grace and mercy towards us is never changing. And he is always there to guide us back into the path of truth. All that he desires of us is that we listen to his voice, hearken to his word, trust in his love, rely on his sufficient grace, and let the love of Christ guard our hearts so that he may direct every step we take for our eternal benefit and his greater glory.
God is willing to speak to us if we are willing to listen.

Confession: Lord, I am willing to listen and obey Your counsel in all things.

February 14

Leviticus 18-19; Matthew 27:32-66

The temple of God

1 Corinthians 3:16-17.
Know ye not that ye are the temple of God, and that the Spirit of God dwelleth in you? If any man defile the temple of God, him shall God destroy; for the temple of God is holy, which temple ye are.

It is a fantastic privilege and a huge responsibility to realize that our frail, human body is the temple of God as Christians. One result of trusting in Jesus as Saviour is to have God's Holy Spirit come and take up permanent residence without our mortal frame. "Do you not know that your body is a temple of the Holy Spirit who is in you, whom you have from God, and that you are not your own? For you have been bought with a price: therefore, glorify God in your body" (1 Corinthians 6:19-20). Just as one must not use his physical body to sin, using this principle, we can say that it is important that we take good care of our body by eating healthy food, exercising, and avoiding harmful things to the body because you are not your own.

Confession: I will not defile the temple of God; I will cultivate a healthy lifestyle.

February 15

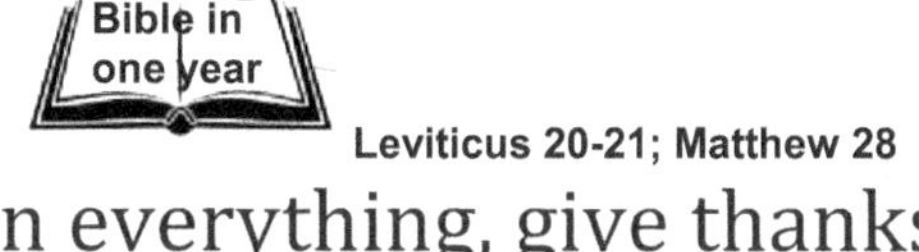

Leviticus 20-21; Matthew 28

In everything, give thanks

1 Thessalonians 5:18
In everything give thanks: for this is the will of God in Christ Jesus concerning you.

Is it possible to give thanks in all circumstances? It seems like God is asking too much of us. Especially during times of great disappointments, tremendous losses, or unbearable heartaches. It's hard for us to comprehend how we are supposed to give thanks during these types of difficulties and challenges. But God is not telling us to be thankful "for" the difficulties. Instead, He wants us to be thankful despite the problems. Thanksgiving provokes God's intervention. We must not let disappointments, failures, losses, and hurts keep us from being grateful to Him. Being thankful in everything starts with the small situations in life, where we can be watchful for everyday issues that trigger ungrateful attitudes, like having a household appliance break down. Thanking God for provision takes the burden off your shoulders in such a situation.

Confession: I will give thanks in all things because it is the will of God.

February 16

Leviticus 22-23; Mark 1:1-22

Health to your flesh

Proverbs 4:21-22

My son, attend to my words; incline thine ear unto my sayings. Let them not depart from thine eyes; keep them in the midst of thine heart. For they are life unto those that find them, and health to all their flesh

I believe that giving attention to the word of God is one of the secrets to living a fruitful life. God's word will help us develop and sustain habits that honour God. It will also allow us to keep our minds on things of God and not on things of this world. The Holy Spirit taught me how to prophesy the scripture. Some years back, while I was having a health issue, I wrote down scriptures on health and prophesied them day and night. It helped me keep God's word in my heart until I got a complete understanding of it (Romans 8:11). I found the truth, and it became health to my flesh. Every negative symptom gradually disappeared when I saw the light. The scripture above says it will be life for those who find them and health to all their flesh. You need to write out the word concerning your situation and prophesy it until you see the light.

Confession: Lord, I receive grace to attend to Your word and keep it in my heart.

February 17

Leviticus 24-25; Mark 1:23-45

Upon Mount Zion

Hebrew 12:22-24
But ye are come unto mount Sion, and unto the city of the living God, the heavenly Jerusalem, and to an innumerable company of angels, To the general assembly and Church of the firstborn, which are written in heaven, and to God the Judge of all, and to the spirits of just men made perfect,And to Jesus the mediator of the new covenant, and to the blood of sprinkling, that speaketh better things than that of Abel.

Yes, we have been translated into the kingdom of God because of our faith in the Lord Jesus Christ. We are now in Mount Zion the city of the living God; we have come to Jesus Christ, our Savior who is interceding for us. His blood is speaking better things for us. His blood speaks forgiveness, healing, mercy, and deliverance. You can stand upon the word of God in Obadiah 1:17 and claim your deliverance because upon mount Zion there shall be deliverance.

Confession: Thank You, Jesus. Your blood is speaking better things for me.

February 18

Leviticus 26-27; Mark 2

He will deliver you

Psalm 34:19
Many are the afflictions of the righteous, But the Lord delivers him out of them all.

The afflictions may be many, but there is deliverance for the righteous. God's people are currently living in a world under the sway of Satan, the wicked one. But our light affliction which is but for a moment is working for us a far more exceeding and eternal weight of glory, (2 Corinthians 4:17). This temporary physical life is a training ground for a beautiful eternity in God's family. We have the authority to resist the devil. We can stand firm in a difficult situation by trusting the Lord for wisdom and strength to endure trials and temptation. God is always with us, and he has assured us that he will deliver us from all afflictions. Your responsibility is to declare his promises and stand firm in the faith.

Confession: Thank You, Father, for Your deliverance.

February 19

Numbers 1-2; Mark 3:1-21

Quick and powerful

Hebrews 4:12

For the word of God is living and powerful, and sharper than any two-edged sword, piercing even to the division of soul and spirit, and of joints and marrow, and is a discerner of the thoughts and intents of the heart.

The Word of God is powerful. It has authority because it is alive and active. When it is declared by faith, it produces life. Many people read the Word of God to acquire basic facts and knowledge about some popular historical facts, and such people will get a mere sense knowledge concept of the Word of God. "Rhema," on the other hand, represents the practical aspect of the word. It is the honey of the word, the spoken word of God to you. A person will never bear good fruit if they only understand the conceptual meaning of God's word. It is necessary to go beyond the logos to the dimension of the Rhema word so that you can maximally benefit from the spiritual impact of the word of God. You only need to ask the Holy Spirit to speak to you as you study the word of God.

Confession: Father, I ask that the Holy Spirit will give me understanding as I study Your word.

February 20

Numbers 3-4; Mark 3:22-35

How to overcome

1 John 5:4
For whatever is born of God overcomes the world. And this is the victory that has overcome the world--our faith.

The Lord Jesus clearly announced, "I have overcome the world." John 16:33. Anyone who puts his faith in the person of Jesus Christ and his finished redemptive work becomes a partaker in Christ's victory over the world and its lusts. The believers in Christ are dead to the world and all its passion and enticements, but alive to God in Christ Jesus. And because the world cannot defile, discourage, distract, influence, or control a dead man, the believers have overcome the world. Your faith is your victory. It is more significant than silver or gold. Hold on to your first love for God. Though the world is full of darkness, you are the light of the world, and you have overcome the darkness of this world through your faith in Christ.

Confession: Thank You, Father, for making me an overcomer.

February 21

Numbers 5-6; Mark 4:1-20

The publishers

Psalm 68:11
The Lord gave the word; Great was the company of those who proclaimed it.

The good news of Jesus is to be proclaimed to all by everyone who confesses his name. He has conquered Satan and death and sin and misery by his death and resurrection. These joyful tidings are to be proclaimed and announced throughout the world. There are various ways we can reveal the good news, through songs, books, messages, or just sharing the testimonies of what God has done for you with your neighbor and family members. Our lives should also proclaim the good news. People should see Jesus in us as Christians through our character and how we relate with other Christians from another denomination. You don't have to be a pastor to proclaim the good news. When the Church leaves the task of evangelism to the ordained offices, the Church will wither and die. The call is for every child of God to go to the world and proclaim the good news that the Lord Jesus has conquered Satan.

Confession: Lord, let my life proclaim the good news.

February 22

Numbers 7; Mark 4:21-41

The Spirit is willing

Matthew 26:41
Watch and pray lest you enter into temptation. The spirit indeed is willing, but the flesh is weak."

Jesus knew that sin had corrupted the nature of man and that the only way to live a victorious life in a fallen world was to watch and pray continuously in utter dependence on the Father through the power of the indwelling Spirit. Keep watching and continuing to pray is the guiding principle for every child of God, every moment of the day, and throughout our time on earth. "Watch and pray that you may not fall into temptation, the spirit in us is willing, but the flesh is weak. However, if we depend on God, abide in Christ, and pray in unity with the Holy Spirit, He will give us the strength to overcome the world, the flesh, and the devil. Christ not only paid the price for our sin but broke the POWER of sin in the lives of all who believe in Jesus Christ.

Confession: Lord, help me to watch and pray always.

February 23

Numbers 8-10; Mark 5:1-21

Your source of strength

Psalm 27:13
I would have lost heart unless I had believed That I would see the goodness of the Lord In the land of the living.

The strength of hope is to believe in the reality of the promises of God. Promises that we cannot yet see with our physical senses, but facts we discern with the eye of faith. That was the trait in David that delighted the Lord. And David proved once again to be a man after God's own heart, a man that trusted the word of the Lord, a man who not only expected God to supply all his needs according to His riches in glory. He believed that God would deliver him from the hands of all his enemies. We too can please God when we unreservedly trust in His Word and believe that he is a God Who rewards those who diligently seek Him and obey His Word in spirit and truth. Today, men's hearts are fearful because of what is going on in the world, but we are not of this world that we should despair, for our faith is in the same God whom David trusted.

Confession: I believe that I will see the goodness of the Lord in the land of the living.

February 24

Numbers 11-13; Mark 5:21-43

Contentment

Psalm 37:16

A little that a righteous man hath Is better than the riches of many wicked.

Sometimes it seems like it doesn't pay to be good! When the evil prospers and the good suffer, we can be tempted to doubt God, especially if we're doing good deeds. If you're not careful to cultivate the proper perspective, you can be tempted to say, "Forget it!" and join the evildoers. When we see the bad guys winning, we need to focus on the Lord. The little that you have is better than the riches of the wicked. God isn't worried about the proud schemes of the wicked. He knows that the seeming victories of the wicked only last for a season, and then their plans will come back on their heads. We are to "rest in the Lord and wait patiently for Him." That's the hard part of the submission. He may not act on your timetable. It may take months, years, or even a whole lifetime for God to work and vindicate you. But if you trust Him to be a just and righteous God and if you submit to Him, then you'll wait patiently.

Confession: Thank You, Father, for Your faithfulness; I am satisfied with You.

February 25

Numbers 14-15; Mark 6:1-32

The voice of God

John 10:27
My sheep hear My voice, and I know them, and they follow Me.

"My sheep hear My voice". This simple Bible verse expresses personal intimacy between the shepherd and his sheep. There has to be a certain familiarity between the sheep and the shepherd which makes the sheep feel safe and know which voice to follow. Jesus said, "I am the good shepherd; I know my sheep and my sheep know me" (John 10:14). Knowing the Lord's voice indicates experiential knowledge through a relationship with Him. We are familiar with the voice of our earthly Father because of the relationship and fellowship we share as a family. So if you want to hear God, get into a deeper relationship with him. The deeper your relationship with God, the more you will be able to recognize his voice.

Confession: Lord draw me nearer to Yourself; I long for a deeper relationship with You.

February 26

Numbers 16-17; Mark 6:33-56

Give me this mountain

Joshua 14:12

Now therefore, give me this mountain of which the Lord spoke in that day; for you heard in that day how the Anakim were there, and that the cities were great and fortified. It may be that the Lord will be with me, and I shall be able to drive them out as the Lord said."

Each of us has a mountain to climb, spiritually speaking. The children of God always face obstacles in their lives. These are distractions, but we can overcome our mountains with His strength no matter how rugged the terrain. Many feel inadequate to face the mountains of life. We learn significant lessons from Caleb as he claimed the promise of God. We find that he was prepared for the task. God provided him with strength for each demand. Caleb had been through the difficult days of the desert. Difficult times strengthen us as we trust God. We lose the fear of hard times because we know that God has previously seen us through hard times. Caleb was determined to stand in the strength of his God.

Confession: Thank You, Father, for the grace and strength to overcome the mountains we encounter each day.

February 27

Numbers 18-20; Mark 7:1-13

We know not

Romans 8:26

Likewise the Spirit also helps in our weaknesses. For we do not know what we should pray for as we ought, but the Spirit Himself makes intercession for us with groanings which cannot be uttered.

As children of God, we have been born from above and have a new human spirit. Before we were born again, our spirit was dead in trespasses and sins. But when we accepted Christ as our Savior, we were given a new life in Christ: a new, human spirit that can commune with His Holy Spirit. We may not know what we should pray for, but the holy spirit helps us as we yield to Him and pray in tongues. He takes over and prays out the will of God for our lives. The Lord instructed us to pray a mysterious prayer in one of our family fasting and prayer time. A mysterious payer is praying in tongues. 1 Corinthians 14:2 says that you are uttering mysteries in the Spirit when praying in tongues.

Confession: Thank You, Father, for the gift of the baptism of the Holy Spirit. I will pray more in tongues.

February 28

Numbers 21-25; Mark 7:14-37; Mark 8:1-21

Beware of Bitterness

Hebrews 12:15
looking carefully lest anyone fall short of the grace of God; lest any root of bitterness springing up cause trouble, and by this many become defiled;

God's grace is always available for us. His grace is the anchor that keeps us strong and focused on Christ. By grace, we grow in faith and the knowledge of God. Remaining steadfast in that grace protects us from harm. Grace protects our hearts from allowing bitterness from situations and experiences to creep in and wreak havoc. The attitude of anger is likened to a bitter root that grows and produces the fruit of its kind. Bitterness will affect your own life. The verse above explains that it will cause trouble and bring defilement when it grows. Many Christians have allowed anger and unforgiveness to grow and produce fruit in their lives. We must remain steadfast in God's grace enabling it to dictate our reaction to all situations.

Confession: I receive grace not to allow bitterness to take root in my life.

March 1

Numbers 26-27; Mark 8:22-38

I will give thee rest

Exodus 33:14
And He said, "My Presence will go with you, and I will give you rest."

When God talks about His presence going with us, He is not referring to some mystical cloud that hovers above us. He is speaking of One, who actively participates in our day-to-day struggles and is the answer for every one of those struggles. We must actively keep ourselves in His presence by maintaining a close relationship with Him throughout the day. God's presence is peace. Most of us have not experienced the full measure of peace in its entirety because we are distracted by the challenges of life. Yet, we have unhindered access to His peace because we have the right to approach God boldly and dwell in His presence. God wants us to be conscious of His divine presence. You can respond to this promise by refusing to give in to anxiety and worry, letting the peace of God reign in your heart. God is with you.

Confession: Lord, I believe that You are always with me. I receive Your rest.

March 2

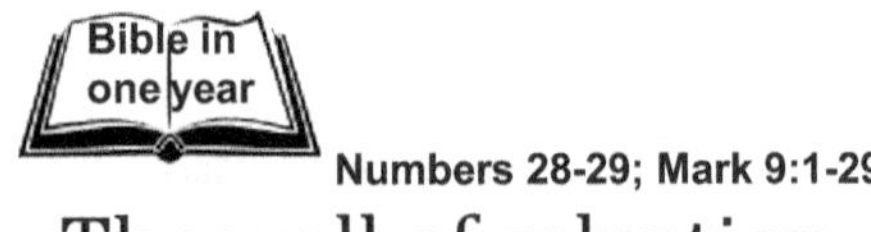

Numbers 28-29; Mark 9:1-29

The well of salvation

Isaiah 12:3
Therefore with joy you will draw water From the wells of salvation.

Sometimes we think of salvation only as that moment when we come to faith in Christ, and He saves us from our sin and guilt once and for all. But that is not all it is. Paul also says in 1 Corinthians 1:18 “To us who *are saved”* the cross is the power of God.
Salvation is a present work of God in our lives. It is going on now, not just in the past. We are saved from troubles daily. The scripture above says that we are to draw from the well of salvation with joy. It means that joy is the rope to pull from the well of salvation. So, we need to maintain a joyful spirit at all times. Even amid adverse situations or circumstances. God will step in and open your eyes to the well of salvation as you avoid murmuring and remain joyful and thankful to Him.

Confession: I will be joyful always because the joy of the Lord is my strength.

March 3

Numbers 30-31; Mark 9:30-50

Love your enemies

Luke 6:35
But love your enemies, do good, and lend, hoping for nothing in return; and your reward will be great, and you will be sons of the Highest. For He is kind to the unthankful and evil

The unusual behaviour and divine love described in this verse can only be manifest in the one born from above, as the life and nature of Christ are manifesting in them. Only those saved by grace through faith in the Lord Jesus can display these divine characteristics of our holy and loving God and Father. Loving those that love us comes naturally, and although there may be a selfish motive underlying human love, Jesus tells us that if you only love those that love you, there is no credit connected with this in God's divine administration. Still, there is an excellent reward for those who love their enemies and friends.

Confession: Lord, I receive grace to love everybody.

March 4

Numbers 32-33; Mark 10:1-31

Keep thy heart

Proverbs 4:23
Keep your heart with all diligence, For out of it spring the issues of life.

When the Bible speaks about the heart, the Bible is not referring to the physical-biological heart that beats. It's referring to the mind, where we have our will and emotions. Mind is where you make your life decisions—every choice you make. Everything you decide to do comes from a decision of your mind. That's why salvation has to be a decision of your mind. To keep your heart means to retain wise words and resist wicked desires. The Bible says as a man thinks in his heart, so is he. You need to declare continually what the word of God says about you. If you confess it long enough, it will become your thought, and when the enemy comes with his lies, your reply will be "it is written," just like Jesus said when He went through temptation.

Confession: I will keep my heart with all diligence. I will be mindful of my thoughts.

March 5

Numbers 34-36; Mark 10:32-52

Stand firm

1 Corinthians 15:58
Therefore, my beloved brethren, be steadfast, immovable, always abounding in the work of the Lord, knowing that your labor is not in vain in the Lord.

Those who believe have a most glorious assurance and thrilling confidence that every promise of God will be fulfilled, including the resurrection of the body and life everlasting. For that reason, we should live in the light of this confident hope. Our trust in God's Word should be steadfast, and our faith in Christ should be immovable, no matter what trials and tribulations we may face. We have to be fruitful in our earthly toil and fulfil the good work that God has given us to do. Let us be committed in the house of God and serve in any of the departments: ushers, protocol, choir, evangelism etc. We need to be occupied at all times in the Lord's work, knowing that our toil is not fruitless in the Lord. There is a reward ahead.

Confession: I am immovable and am committed to God's work; there is a reward awaiting me.

March 6

Deuteronomy 1-2; Mark 11:1-19

They shall be filled

Matthew 5:6
Blessed are those who hunger and thirst for righteousness, For they shall be filled.

Our heavenly Father is a God of righteousness and in Christ, we are clothed with His character. In the power of the Holy Spirit, we are being changed into His likeness and conformed more and more into His image as we spend time with Him. How blessed are those that hunger and thirst for the righteousness of Christ, for they shall indeed be satisfied. Our desire and craving should not be more of our righteousness and religious activities, for as the bible says, our own righteousness is as filthy rags to the Lord. Our hunger and thirst should be for more of Christ, that we may grow in grace and the knowledge of our Lord Jesus. As we yield our lives to the Holy Spirit, He will conform us to become more and more like Christ.

Confession: Lord, help me to grow in grace and in the knowledge of our Lord Jesus Christ.

March 7

Deuteronomy 3-4; Mark 11:20-33

Faith and good conscience

1 Timothy 1:19
Holding faith and a good conscience; which some have put away concerning faith, have made shipwreck.

In this bible verse, Paul is instructing his disciple Timothy on living a Christian life that is pleasing to God. This warning is for us as Christians; only those who live by faith are pleasing to God, while those who try to live their Christian life in any other way will shipwreck their faith. They will live a fleshly life that is not pleasing to the Lord and thereby fall from grace. To live by faith is to believe in His word. If you believe, you will not worry about anything. The second thing mentioned in the scripture above is that we maintain a good conscience; the book of Romans 13:8 says we should owe no man anything but to love one another. Let us not be those who shipwreck their faith by deliberately refusing to do the right thing; instead, let us run the race that is set before us and cling more tightly to our faith.

Confession: Lord, help me to please You daily by walking in faith and maintaining a good conscience.

March 8

Deuteronomy 5-7; Mark 12:1-27

The Lord was with him

Genesis 39:21
But the Lord was with Joseph and showed him mercy, and He gave him favor in the sight of the keeper of the prison.

This scripture reminds me of the contrast between Joseph and his brothers. The brothers were not sold as slaves but were sleeping in their beds among their own families. The brothers seem to be free, but they were slaves to secrets, shame, and guilt. They were in bondage, but Joseph was a slave, but free, he refused to soil his hands with sin, and God was with him. Let God be with you no matter the circumstance. Joseph found favor in the prison because of God's blessing and Joseph's faithfulness. God made sure Joseph was advanced in his position, even as a slave. It took 11 years for the full measure of God's blessing to be accomplished in Joseph's life.
Many think if advancement is from God, it must come quickly, But sometimes God allows good things to develop slowly. Just wait for Him.

Confession: Thank You, Lord, for being with me. I receive grace to live a holy life.

March 9

Deuteronomy 8-10; Mark 12:28-44

What are you saying?

Mark 11:23
For assuredly, I say to you, whoever says to this mountain, 'Be removed and be cast into the sea,' and does not doubt in his heart, but believes that those things he says will be done, he will have whatever he says.

"And does not doubt" How is such undoubting faith possible? The only way we can have undoubting faith is to know God's will in a particular situation. How do we determine what God intends to do in response to faith? There are two answers: one is that God reveals His will through the scripture, the other is that God can show His intention apart from scripture privately to an individual or group. You can respond to the scripture above by saying what His word says concerning you. I always prophesy the revealed will (the scripture) concerning any issue until I receive light. Keep saying what you believe on purpose. Take it like medicine day and night. Your victory is sure.

Confession: I will keep saying what Your word says concerning me regardless of the situation.

March 10

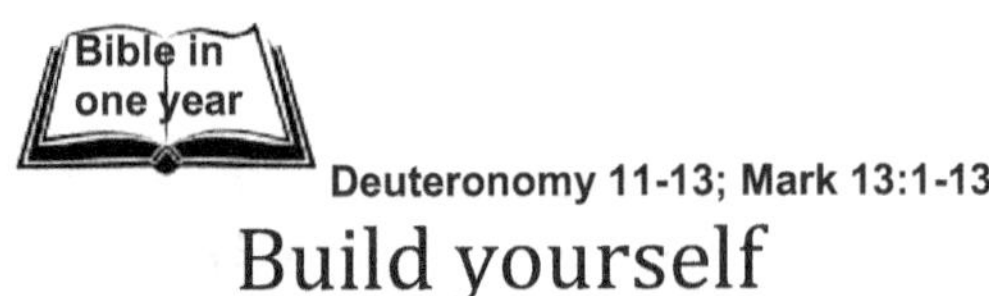

Deuteronomy 11-13; Mark 13:1-13

Build yourself

Jude 1:20
But you, beloved, building yourselves up on your most holy faith, praying in the Holy Spirit.

We are in a time wherein people are departing from the faith and will not put up with wholesome teaching at all. We need to build our confidence to stand firm in times like this. We are to pray in the Spirit, which means that we are to lay aside our fleshly nature and allow the Holy Spirit to pray out the will of God. Praying in tongues activates the power of God in us. It builds our spiritual muscles and opens us up to divine mysteries. Apostle Paul said in Romans 8:26, " Likewise the Spirit also helps in our weaknesses. For we do not know what we should pray for as we ought, but the Spirit Himself makes intercession for us with groanings which cannot be uttered". Praying in tongues is the key to unlock divine mysteries. The more you pray in tongues, the more His divine direction gets clearer. It helps you to download God's plan for your life.

Confession: I will build up myself daily by praying in the Spirit.

March 11

Deuteronomy 14-16; Mark 13:14-37

The angels are waiting

Psalm 103:20
Bless the LORD, ye his angels, that excel in strength, that do his commandments, hearkening unto the voice of his word.

Yes, the angels are waiting for you to give them the word of God to execute. When believers declare the word of God, the angels listen to them and will not allow the words to fall to the ground. We have to understand that if we don't give voice to the word of God on earth, then the angels have no voice to listen to. Many today are missing out on some incredible benefits because they are not giving voice to God's word. Instead, they are voicing out fear, unbelief, negative messages they hear from the news etc. They believe in the report of the world and neglect the report of God. A songwriter wrote, "I'm not moved by what I hear, see or feel, but I'm only moved by the word of God." Whose report do you believe?

Concession: I will consciously give voice to the word of God that I believe.

March 12

Deuteronomy 17-19; Mark 14:1-25

I have found a ransom

Job 33:24-25

Then he is gracious unto him, and saith, Deliver him from going down to the pit: I have found a ransom. His flesh shall be fresher than a child's: he shall return to the days of his youth:

"I have found a ransom." Oh, what a glorious revelation! This is none other than Jesus Christ, whom the Father found in the counsels of eternity as the surety of the covenant. Our Redeemer, the Deliverer of the elect. Christ is the Purchaser and the Price, the Sacrifice, Priest, and All in all. "Forasmuch then as the children are partakers of flesh and blood, He also Himself likewise took part of the same; that through death He might destroy him that had the power of death, that is, the devil, and deliver them who through fear of death were all their lifetime subject to bondage." (Heb. 2:14,15) I always declare (Job 33:24-25) everyday in my quit time.

Confession: My flesh is fresher than a child's.I shall return to the days of my youth.

March 13

Deuteronomy 20-22; Mark 14:26-50

The eyes of your understanding

Ephesians 1:18
The eyes of your understanding being enlightened; that ye may know what is the hope of his calling, and what the riches of the glory of his inheritance in the saints.

Paul prays that God will enlighten our hearts so that we may know the hope of God's calling, the hope to which He has called us. We need to keep our hopes alive by looking unto Jesus. We are all waiting for the coming of the Lord, but it doesn't really turn us on very much. We know it as a doctrine, but it isn't very exciting. The scripture guarantees this hope. It is a hope that we should be excited about. It gives us the certainty that we will one day live in heaven as a new creature and that on earth we will be men and women filled with the Spirit of God, which enables us to mount up with wings like the eagle, a soul that can run and not be weary, a body which can walk and not faint. When our eyes of understanding are enlightened, we will know the hope of his calling. We will understand the scripture better.

Confession: Father, I pray that You will enlighten my eyes of understanding.

March 14

Deuteronomy 23-25; Mark 14:51-72

Restoration

Joel 2:25

So I will restore to you the years that the swarming locust has eaten, The crawling locust, The consuming locust, And the chewing locust, My great army which I sent among you.

This tremendous promise for us as children of God means that the years of abundant harvests would follow the years of desolation brought about by the locusts. Examples of lost years are fruitless years, painful years, misdirected years, rebellious years, Christ-less years, etc. Ask anyone who came to faith in Christ later in life. Such people will tell you that they wish they had come to Christ sooner than they did. Still, God has promised restoration. He can restore the years you have lost by deepening your communion with Christ, multiplying your fruitfulness, and bringing long-term gain from short-term loss. He is a faithful God.

Confession: Thank You, Lord. I believe You will restore all the fruitless years.

March 15

Deuteronomy 26-27; Mark 15:1-26

Due season

Galatians 6:9
And let us not grow weary while doing good, for in due season we shall reap if we do not lose heart.

The simple gospel of grace requires no effort for we are saved by grace simply through faith in Christ Jesus, but living our Christian life as unto the Lord requires patience and endurance, as we press on, day by day in the footsteps of our Saviour, to the goal of our calling, which is to be conformed into the image of Christ. It takes effort and courage that only comes from the Spirit of God. Joseph was in prison, yet he was doing good (Genesis 39). His due season came years later, and he was greatly rewarded. The Bible says that the Lord's word tried him (Psalm 105:19). Keep doing well even when people reward you with evil, and your heavenly Father will reward you abundantly in due season.

Confession: I receive grace not to grow weary in doing good. God will reward me in due season.

March 16

Deuteronomy 28; Mark 15:27-47

He will instruct you

Psalm 32:8
I will instruct you and teach you in the way you should go; I will guide you with My eye.

God is willing to instruct and teach us if we can walk in His ways. Like many of us, David chose to do the evil and refused the good. David knew the Word of God forbade adultery and murder, but he decided to embrace his fleeting passion and lost his special connection with the Lord. I have discovered that unconfessed sin haunts the conscience of a believer and contributes to health problems and heavy-heartedness. When David stopped hiding his sin and said, "I will confess my transgressions to the LORD," that God forgave the guilt of his sin and promised to instruct and teach him. When lessons have been learned, and fellowship is restored, God always brings us closer in communion with Himself.

Confession: Lord, help me embrace Your ways and enjoy Your guidance daily.

March 17

Deuteronomy 29-30; Mark 16

Fear not

Isaiah 41:10
Fear not, for I am with you; Be not dismayed, for I am your God. I will strengthen you, Yes, I will help you, I will uphold you with My righteous right hand.'

These comforting words "Fear Not" appears in the Bible 366 times, one for each day of the year, plus one for each leap year. But no matter how many times these words of encouragement appear, it will be of no benefit to us if we don't have faith in His word and refuse to fear. Unless we trust His word, we can't please Him. We are not to worry, for He has promised to strengthen all that is His. He will be an ever-present help in trouble. Indeed, the Lord Jesus Himself promised, Lo I am with you always, even to the end of the age, and He even sent His indwelling Holy Spirit to be our present Helper and our resident Comforter at all times and in all places.

Confession: Thank You, Father, for being with me. I will not fear.

March 18

Deuteronomy 31-32; Luke 1:1-23

Subdue and dominate

Genesis 1:28
Then God blessed them, and God said to them, "Be fruitful and multiply; fill the earth and subdue it; have dominion over the fish of the sea, over the birds of the air, and over every living thing that moves on the earth."

The man was the crowning glory of God's entire creation, and as husband and wife, Adam and Eve were authorized to rule over the works of God's hands, for God had put all rule and authority under the feet of His representative. Remarkably, God trusts us to carry out this incredible task of building on the good earth He has given us. A good question is whether we *are* working more productively and beautifully. History is full of examples of people whose Christian faith resulted in extraordinary accomplishments. An essential aspect of God at work in creation is the vast imagination that could create everything. You can use the power of imagination and create your desired future.

Confession: I will be fruitful; I will be more productive.

March 19

Deuteronomy 33-34; Luke 1:24-56

Platform for increase

Psalm 67:5-6

Let the peoples praise You, O God; Let all the peoples praise You. Then the earth shall yield her increase; God, our own God, shall bless us.

What happens when we praise God? "*Then shall the earth yield her increase, and God, even our own God, shall bless us.*" Our unthankfulness is the cause of the earth's unfruitfulness. When we praise God, He blesses us with His goodness. God *created* us to know His way, His salvation, and His praise. When we choose to live by these desires of God, the earth itself is happy because the people of the planet are doing what God created them to do. God's natural order for creation and humankind is then honoured, and blessing is the result. It is just like using something for the exact use and how the manufacturer designed it. Complaining and murmuring leads to destruction but thanksgiving and praise help us live a worry-free life. Just keep thanking and praising Him even in the wilderness.

Confession: Lord, I receive grace to praise You continually.

March 20

Joshua 1-3; Luke 1:57-8

The battleground

2 Corinthians 10:4-5

For the weapons of our warfare are not carnal but mighty in God for pulling down strongholds, casting down arguments and every high thing that exalts itself against the knowledge of God, bringing every thought into captivity to the obedience of Christ.

The weapons of Christian warfare are divinely powerful for the destruction of fortresses. Paul explained that in this Church age, we do not use carnal weapons because we are in a spiritual battle and require spiritual weapons. But unfortunately, many Christians are using a carnal weapon to fight: malice, unforgiveness, revenge. These are all carnal weapons. Sometimes we go as far as confronting people physically because we saw them in the dream. We are to use the word of God to cast down all these imaginations planted by the enemy from our minds. We are to bring them to the obedience of Christ by choosing to do what God said in His word.

Confession: I pull down every stronghold, and I bring them to the obedience of God's word.

March 21

Joshua 4-6; Luke 2:1-24

The cry for mercy

Matthew 9:27
When Jesus departed from there, two blind men followed Him, crying out and saying, "Son of David, have mercy on us!"

"Have mercy on us, Son of David!" It is a simple sentence but full of deep meaning. Notice first of all that their cry was for mercy. A request for mercy is a request to get something good that you don't deserve. These two blind men were crying out to Jesus for mercy because they knew they were not deserving of His help. They also cried out to Jesus because they knew that He could help them. Jesus asked them in verse 28, do you believe that I can do this? They said to Him," yes, Lord" They got what they asked for. In verse 29, Jesus said, "according to your faith be it unto you." Do you believe that God can help you?. It will be unto you, according to your faith.

Confession: Have mercy on me, oh Lord, my help is from You alone.

March 22

Joshua 7-8; Luke 2:25-52

His dwelling place

Psalm 22:3
But You are holy, Enthroned in the praises of Israel.

David is expressing in this Messianic psalm the power-packed expression that God is holy, and He is exalted in praises. This is the kind of faith that sings in times of difficulty. In verse one, he was roaring, but there was no answer. In verse 2, he cried, but there was no answer, but in verse three, he lifted his voice in praise to the highest God who can deliver him from all troubles. He promised to keep on declaring the goodness of God. You might have cried and prayed about the situation, but now it is time to give Him sacrificial praise. We are to praise God always, both in good and challenging times because God dwells in our praises and His presence is enough to handle the situation at hand.

Confession: Lord, you are holy. I will praise You forever.

March 23

Joshua 9-10; Luke 3

Obedience

Hebrew 11:7
By faith Noah, being divinely warned of things not yet seen, moved with godly fear, prepared an ark for the saving of his household, by which he condemned the world and became heir of the righteousness which is according to faith.

Noah was warned by God about things never before seen. Noah's obedient faith is recorded, and God remembers him as an heir of righteousness. Faith dwells in the inner heart, but obedience is the observable external manifestation of faith. Steadfast obedience over time during difficult and incomprehensible circumstances, despite the opposition and rejection of others, follows the example of Christ and will ultimately result in incredible blessings from God. Your calling may not be like that of Noah, but the little things He is asking you to do, how obedient are you to His call? How are you responding to that inner, still small voice within your heart?

Confession: Help me, Lord, to obey You in all things.

March 24

Joshua 11-13; Luke 4:1-32

He is working in you

Philippians 2:13
For it is God who works in you both to will and to do for His good pleasure.

Once we accept Christ by faith and receive the gift of eternal life, repenting of our sins and turning to God, we become disciples of Jesus. God has a plan for each one of us according to His "good purpose," and He will not fail to fulfill it. When we work towards godliness, God, by His Holy Spirit, works in and through us. It is definitely by our "will," but God works in us to will. With the gentle prompting of the Holy Spirit, we are willing to work out our salvation, thanking God, who has given us the grace to do so. God has a plan in everything that He does through and in us. He has plans for our life, and they are good. Everything that we go through in this life as we follow Christ, though painful sometimes, should be considered good because all things work together for good to those who love God.

Confession: Thank You, Father, for placing it in my heart to do those things that are perfect in Christ.

March 25

Joshua 14-15; Luke 4:33-44

Good measure

Luke 6:38
Give, and it will be given to you: good measure, pressed down, shaken together, and running over will be put into your bosom. For with the same measure that you use, it will be measured back to you."

In this verse, Jesus beautifully expands the fundamental principles of sowing and reaping. He teaches that generous or unselfish people will not only benefit from the generosity and graciousness of others, but that people will pour into their lives a good measure pressed down, shaken together, and running over. However, the universal principle of sowing and reaping does not necessarily refer to material benefits. We are urged to lay for ourselves treasure in heaven, where moth and rust cannot damage and thieves cannot break in and steal.

Confession: Lord, I receive grace to be generous and show love to people.

March 26

Joshua 16-18; Luke 5:1-16

Wait for Him

Lamentations 3:25-26
The Lord is good to those who wait for Him, To the soul who seeks Him. It is good that one should hope and wait quietly For the salvation of the Lord.

God is good to those that wait for Him, to those that submit to His perfect will. To those who trust in His unfailing word. God is good to the person who searches for Him, for He is not far from any of us, and we will find Him if we search for Him with all our hearts. It means thatyour heart is fixed, there is no room for compromise, you are ready to wait on God no matter how long it takes. The secret to a victorious life is to submit to the ways and workings of the Lord, to yield to His tests inlife, and to surrender to His rod of chastening so that like Job, we can say, "When He has tried me, I shall come forth as gold."

Confession: I will wait on You, Lord. You are the very present help in times of trouble.

March 27

Joshua 19-20; Luke 5:17-39

Through knowledge

2 Peter 1:3
as His divine power has given to us all things that pertain to life and godliness, through the knowledge of Him who called us by glory and virtue.

God is working in us to get us matured in our faith, grow in grace, and come into a fuller and more profound knowledge of our Lord and Savior, Jesus Christ. It is only by God's divine power that we are saved through faith in Christ's sacrificial work at Calvary, and it is only by God's divine power that we are enabled to live our Christian life as unto the Lord. We have been given all things necessary for a vibrant spiritual life; We have access to these blessings through the knowledge of God. The closer you are to God through fellowship and the study of His word, the more like Him you become, and you will be able to access all that is yours in Christ Jesus.

Confession: Thank You, Lord, for giving me all things. I receive grace to access them in Jesus.

March 28

Joshua 21-22; Luke 6:1-26

My Help

Psalm 121:2-3
My help comes from the Lord, Who made heaven and earth. He will not allow your foot to be moved; He who keeps you will not slumber.

Our help comes from the Lord, the Maker of heaven and earth. We need to declare this word of God daily, for we know that our strength, support, provision, and protection came only from the Lord. We are not required to visit Jerusalem for forgiveness and mercy, as some people do, for we have the Spirit of God residing forever in our hearts. By the sacrifice of Christ's blood, we have access into the holy throne-room of God every moment of the day. Praise God that we can come boldly to the throne of grace to obtain mercy. He has promised never to leave us nor forsake us but will be our ever-present help.

Confession: Thank You, Father, for Your mercies. They are new every morning.

March 29

Joshua 23-24; Luke 6:27-49

The anointing teaches you

John 2:27
But the anointing which you have received from Him abides in you, and you do not need that anyone teach you; but as the same anointing teaches you concerning all things, and is true, and is not a lie, and just as it has taught you, you will abide in Him.

By grace through faith in Christ's sacrificial work at Calvary, each of us receives the anointing of the Holy Spirit at salvation when He comes to indwell us and abide in us permanently. This anointing is given the moment we trust Christ for our salvation, for we were bought with a price, the precious blood of Jesus Christ, and the cost of our redemption was paid in full at Calvary. Having received the anointing of God, the indwelling Spirit, and the abiding life of Christ Jesus our Lord, every believer has an assurance that those who walk in spirit and truth will be guided into all truth. We can get confirmation from a prophet or anyone, but your conviction must be by the Holy Spirit living inside of you.

Confession: Thank You, Lord, for the indwelling presence of the Holy Spirit Who is teaching us all things.

March 30

Judges 1-2; Luke 7:1-30

Not by works

Titus 3:5
not by works of righteousness which we have done, but according to His mercy He saved us, through the washing of regeneration and renewing of the Holy Spirit,

Our salvation is NOT because of work of righteousness that we had done, but according to His mercy; we are a new creature in Christ through the Holy Spirit from the moment we receive salvation. God's mercy was poured out on us richly through Jesus Christ. God is rich in mercy; he is not willing that any should perish but that all should come to repentance and turn from their sins. He is ready to wash away our sins and give us new life in Christ by the power of His Holy Spirit. The one and only 'condition' is to believe in the Lord Jesus Christ and be baptized; you will be saved, and you will be preserved in troubles of life through your faith in His promises.

Confession: Thank you, Lord, for saving me. I will forever be grateful.

March 31

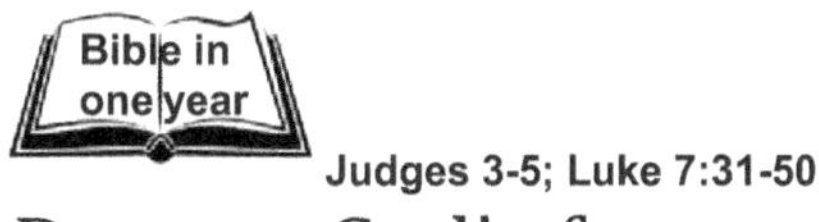

Judges 3-5; Luke 7:31-50

Door to God's favour

Proverbs 3:3-4
Let not mercy and truth forsake you; Bind them around your neck, Write them on the tablet of your heart, and so find favor and high esteem In the sight of God and man.

"Let not mercy and truth forsake you," This means when you embrace these two qualities, they will open the door to God's favour upon your life. Another translation says love and faithfulness. Favour (trustworthiness/Truth) and steadfast love characterize God's behaviour toward His people. And in return, since covenants are reciprocal, His people are expected to return faithfulness and true love to Him and our neighbour. We need to be faithful in gathering together with other believers and be willing to serve in the house of God. People should see Christ in us as believers. Our lives should be worthy of emulation.

Confession: Help me, Lord, to live a life of faithfulness and love.

April 1

Judges 6-7; Luke 8:1-21

He knows what to do

John 6:6
But this He said to test him, for He Himself knew what He would do. When Jesus then lifted up his eyes, and saw a great company come unto him, he saith unto Philip, Whence shall we buy bread, that these may eat?

Jesus asks the disciples how they will solve the problem of a hungry crowd to test their faith. Unlike the devil, who uses challenges and tests to entangle us in sin. God's tests are meant to refine our faith. Jesus already knew what He would do about the problem, but He wanted to know how far they had grown in their faith. Jesus wanted to see and hear from the disciples where they would turn to for answers in such a situation. It is just like sitting for an exam after you have received lectures. The disciple still focused on human efforts, whereas Jesus' resolution began with reliance and gratitude to God. This reliance on God, first and foremost, is a lesson we should hold on to.

Confession: Thank You, Father, You can perfect all that concerns me.

April 2

Judges 8-9; Luke 8:22-56

There is lifting

Job 22:29
When men are cast down, then thou shalt say, There is lifting up; and he shall save the humble person.

The saints can still place their hope in God, who is faithful, good, holy, immutable, intelligent, just, knowledgeable, loving, merciful, moral, omniscient, omnipotent, and omnipresent. We can determinedly and devotedly place our hope in God to lift us even when the whole world is crying and searching for a solution. The scripture above says that God will save the humble person. Why? Because it takes humility to believe the report of the Lord regardless of what is happening around you. By faith, you can say "there is lifting" because you believe that His hands are not shortened that He cannot save. God is committed to doing what you are saying. We must choose our words wisely.

Confession: There is lifting for me in Jesus' name.

April 3

Bible in one year

Judges 10-11; Luke 9:1-36

Above all else

Proverbs 4:23
Keep your heart with all diligence, For out of it spring the issues of life.

According to the Bible, to guard our hearts, we must protect the truths and biblical instructions given to us by the Holy Spirit. The lies in the heart make a fool to do terrible things. The fool says in his heart, 'There is no God.' They are corrupt; they do abominable deeds; there is none who does good" psalm 14:1. Throughout the Scripture, we can see that guarding one's heart means making sure you are careful to live according to God's word. To guard your heart means that you fill it with truth, and then you make sure you guard that truth, so you do not forget it or ignore it. Your heart is the place where your identity is housed, "As in water face reflects face, so the heart of man reflects the man" (Proverbs 27:19).

Confession: Lord, I receive grace to guard my heart with all diligence.

April 4

Judges 12-14; Luke 9:37-62

Hold on to your confession

Hebrews 4:14
Seeing then that we have a great High Priest who has passed through the heavens, Jesus the Son of God, let us hold fast our confession.

We believe with the heart and with the mouth, confession is made unto salvation (Romans 10:9-10). The way we became Christian is the same way we are to possess all our rights and privileges in Christ. The above scripture encourages us to hold on to our confession. When you declare the word of God over your life, you are enforcing the truth, and you are also releasing life to the situation at hand. Jesus said, "the words that I speak to you they are spirit and they are life" (John 6:63). Let us work out our salvation by declaring our rights and privileges in Christ on purpose, holding on to the confession of God's faithfulness in our lives. Our confession of God's promises should continue till we receive our salvation.

Confession: I will daily declare my rights and privileges in Christ on purpose.

April 5

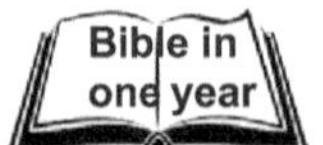

Judges 15-17; Luke 10:1-24

The spirit of revelation

Ephesians 1:17
That the God of our Lord Jesus Christ, the Father of glory, may give to you the spirit of wisdom and revelation in the knowledge of Him.

There is so much that God wants to communicate to us through the Holy Spirit. Paul here prays that God will grant us the capacity to receive and understand it. God wants us to know Him intimately, and because His ways are so unfathomable, He has given us the Holy Spirit to enable us to come into that continual revelation. The idea behind the word revelation means uncovering or unveiling. It is used in several ways, but here it is used to communicate the knowledge of God to the soul. The word "in the knowledge of Him" denotes exact or complete knowledge, expressing a full understanding by the "knower," which powerfully influences them. This prayer is for us. We need to ask God for the spirit of wisdom and revelation.

Confession: Lord, I ask for the spirit of wisdom and revelation.

April 6

Judges 18-19; Luke 10:25-42

The lonely

Psalm 68:6
God sets the solitary in families; He brings out those who are bound into prosperity; But the rebellious dwell in a dry land.

Have there been times in your life that you feel all alone? Yes, I have been there. I remember feeling so lonely in my teen years when my senior brother died in a motor accident. Being an orphan, he was like a father to me. Though friends and church members were around me, I felt so lonely inside. I can tell you that you can be lonely and have a lot of friends. You can be lonely and be around a lot of people. If you have ever gone through a divorce or disappointment, you might have experienced loneliness. But if you can cry out to God in total dependence, He will heal your heart and surround you with lovely people. God knows that in isolation, we do no one any good. He puts the lonely in families.

Confession: Thank you Lord, for being so faithful.

April 7

Judges 20-21; Luke 11:1-28

Give no place

Ephesians 4:26-27

Be ye angry, and sin not: let not the sun go down upon your wrath: Neither give place to the devil.

"Do not give the devil an opportunity." This is Paul's plea to these Christians in Ephesus and his earnest appeal to each member of the Body of Christ today. The word "place" carries the meaning of "power, or an opportunity." It is the idea of giving someone a secure foothold from which further progress can be made. 1 Peter 5:8 says, your adversary the devil, as a roaring lion, walketh about, seeking whom he may devour. The moment we find ourselves "open" to any sin or disobedience, it will not be long before our enemy has stolen our happiness, holiness, and honour away from us. Eli left an evil door open to his sons, and sorrow moved in. Gehazi left the door of greed open, and the shame of leprosy moved in. You can never give the devil a foot that he doesn't end up taking a mile! Consider the consequences of giving place to the devil through anger or any ungodly attitude.

Confession: I will not give place to the devil in my life in Jesus' name.

April 8

Ruth 1-4; Luke 11:29-54

In time of trouble

Psalm 27:4-5
One thing I have desired of the Lord, That will I seek: That I may dwell in the house of the Lord All the days of my life, To behold the beauty of the Lord, And to inquire in His temple. For in the time of trouble He shall hide me in His pavilion; In the secret place of His tabernacle He shall hide me; He shall set me high upon a rock.

How do we live with confidence? How can we know we can stay on track? Where can we turn for hope and reassurance? David declared in the scripture above that the most important thing to him was to seek the presence of God continually and meditate in His word. That is the only secure place in a noisy world. Many folks are trying to keep their lives moving without God on board. We need daily directions to see our way clear. For David, worship was an essential discipline. Just as God helped him find his way through dark times, God will also help us through dark times.

Confession: I will seek after You Lord, Your presence is all I need.

April 9

1 Samuel 1-3; Luke 12:1-34

Blossom

Isaiah 35:2
The wilderness and the solitary place shall be glad for them; and the desert shall rejoice, and blossom as the rose.

This promise is for us today. God will bring a beautiful restoration to His people. Just like God's people in exile, we have our own wilderness experiences, and each one of us yearns for a way through the issues of life. God does not eliminate wilderness from our lives, but He changes those scary spaces by being present within us. Those chaotic and confusing spaces may exist; however, God changes how we see and experience them. From hopeless to potential and possibility, from exhaustion and despair to renewed energy and anticipation. We need to open our eyes to see God's presence and guidance on the journey of life.

Confession: I will rejoice and blossom. This is my time of restoration.

April 10

1 Samuel 4-6; Luke 12:35-59

Strong faith

Romans 4:19
And not being weak in faith, he did not consider his own body, already dead (since he was about a hundred years old), and the deadness of Sarah's womb.

Abrahams's faith is an example to us all. Even when his body and his wife were incapable of producing a child, he believed in God's promise that they would have a son. If God told you that a 100-year-old man and a 90-year-old woman would have a child, would you believe it? Faith believes what cannot be seen or reasoned with the natural mind. Faith pleases God (Hebrews 11:6). Maybe you feel as if a giant is facing you. It can be financial, vocational, relational problems looming large before you. You can take your eyes off your limitations and put them on the limitless one. The truth is that when faith comes, fear flees. When we start worshipping, our faith begins to grow. That is why worship is so important. Not only does it bless the Father, but it also feeds our faith.

Confession: I am strong in faith, giving glory to God always.

April 11

1 Samuel 7-9; Luke 13:1-21

Tell people about Jesus

John 1:40-41

One of the two which heard John speak, and followed him, was Andrew, Simon Peter's brother.He first findeth his own brother Simon, and saith unto him, We have found the Messias, which is, being interpreted, the Christ.

Andrew realized that he should share the good news with his brother, Simon. He pointed his brother to the One who could change him and satisfy all his needs. This is what we all as Christians should be doing, telling people about Christ. How many people have you brought to Jesus? Are you ashamed of Him? I remember sharing my salvation story with a dear friend living in another city. I simply wrote a letter and shared my new faith in Christ. Years later, I learned that my story got him to his knees, and he gave his life to Jesus after reading the letter. Just keep on sharing your story. It's a seed.

Confession: I will testify of your salvation Lord. I will not be ashamed.

April 12

1 Samuel 10-12; Luke 13:22-35

What are you hearing

Mark 5:27
When she heard about Jesus, she came behind Him in the crowd and touched His garment.

Faith is like a switch that ignites the power of God to flow out. When the button of faith is turned on, the power of God is released to handle the situation at hand. The scripture above says that she heard of Jesus, heard of the healing miracles. She was fully persuaded that a touch of His garment would make her whole. She took action to actualize her desire. The lesson from her story is that we keep hearing the word of God concerning the issue day and night until we are fully persuaded. Then we can step out in faith and do as the Holy Spirit instructs us. You need to sit down and feed your faith by hearing the word of God.

Confession: I will give more time to hear the word of God to release the power of faith within.

April 13

1 Samuel 13-14; Luke 14:1-24

The fig tree

Mark 11:21
And Peter, remembering, said to Him, "Rabbi, look! The fig tree which You cursed has withered away."

The words that Jesus spoke to the fig tree in mark 11:14 took effect immediately, but the leaves were still green. The following morning Peter called the attention of Jesus that the fig tree had withered. The truth is, it withered the same hour Jesus cursed it. But the physical manifestation took some time. The word of faith we speak over our situations is effective but needs time to manifest physically, so don't look at the green leaves. Don't look at the symptoms and pains you feel. The root is already dead. It's a matter of time. You will see the manifestation. Concentrate on the word even if the symptom persists. "Looking unto Jesus the Author and the Finisher of our faith."

Confession: I will keep my eyes on the word, not the symptoms.

April 14

1 Samuel 15-16; Luke 14:25-35

The measure of Christ gift

Ephesians 4:7
But to each one of us grace was given according to the measure of Christ's gift.

It is in Him that we live and move and have our being, and it is through Him, that we have been made a New Creation in Christ. By His grace, through faith in Him, we have been granted theforgiveness of sin and life everlasting.
In addition to all the fantastic privileges, we have already been granted grace. The Lord has bestowed on His blood-bought children His unmerited grace and favour on each of His children. To each one of us, grace was given according to the measure of Christ's gift. It took quite a great effort to write this devotional manual, but the grace of God upon me did it all as I released myself to be used of God. The grace of God upon you is waiting to be released.

Confession: Thank you, Father, for Your grace. I will release Your gift in me to bless the world.

April 15

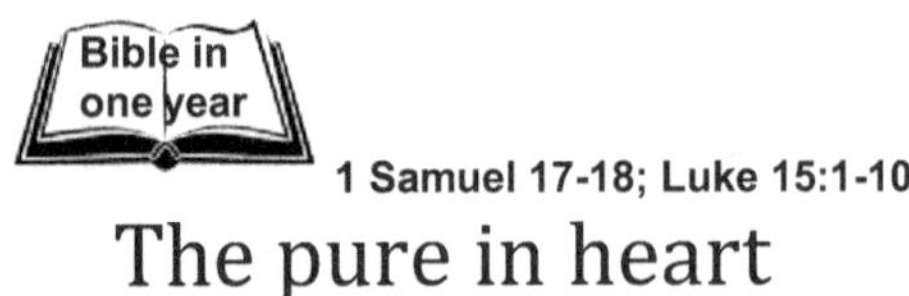

1 Samuel 17-18; Luke 15:1-10

The pure in heart

Matthew 5:8

Blessed are the pure in heart, For they shall see God.

The purity of the heart of which Jesus speaks is the purity that comes from the purifying work ofthe new covenant. Only with pure hearts, cleansed by the blood of Jesus, can men pursue holiness and purity. God purifies our hearts by giving us a new affection for Him and a new set of appetites for His word. The word of God is a fountain of delights that cleanses us continually. Jesus said, “Sanctify them through thy truth: thy word is truth.” God opens our eyes to behold the splendor of His glory (2 Cor 4:6), and when He does, He circumcises our hearts and replaces vile unbelief with a simple, pure trust in Him.

Despite our struggle with the flesh, we can still find true purity by setting our eyes on Christ.

Confession: Lord, I receive grace to cleanse my heart continually through Your word.

April 16

1 Samuel 19-21; Luke 15:11-32

Rest in the Lord

Psalm 37:7
Rest in the Lord, and wait patiently for Him; Do not fret because of him who prospers in his way, Because of the man who brings wicked schemes to pass.

Being still in the presence of God is not a sulky silence or hushed murmuring but is simply resting in Him, trusting in His Word of truth, abiding in His love, and being patient to wait for His timing. It is to possess purposeful patience and not display a glum resignation. When we are quietly resting in His presence and secure in the hope set before us, the peace of God which passes understanding will flood the heart and soul of all who walk godly in Christ Jesus. Let us daily be still in the presence of the LORD as we wait patiently for Him to act. Let us not worry about evil people who prosper nor fret about their wicked schemes, for they will eventually be cut off.

Confession: I will rest in the Lord and wait patiently for Him.

April 17

1 Samuel 22-24; Luke 16:1-18

A new commandment

John 13:34
A new commandment I give to you, that you love one another; as I have loved you, that you also love one another.

No one can love as Christ loved in the power of their own sinful flesh. No one can love as Jesus loved by their imperfect human effort, however hard they try, for the love of man is but a faint reflection of the glorious Son of Righteousness. But all who trust in His name have been made a new creation. We have the life of Christ living in us and through us. And only as we walk in spirit and submission to the leading of the Holy Spirit can we fulfil this beautiful command to love. Until we can at last say with Paul, "it is not I that lives but Christ that lives in me." We need to allow the love of God, which is shed abroad in our hearts by the Holy Spirit, to flow out to others.

Confession: Thank You, Father, for Your love. I receive grace to allow the love of God to flow through me.

April 18

1 Samuel 25-26; Luke 16:19-31

Let this mind be in you

Philippians 2:5
Let this mind be in you, which was also in Christ Jesus:

The joy of the Lord is indeed our strength, and we are called to rejoice evermore, pray without ceasing; give thanks in all things, and live in unity with one another. But we can only do this as we allow the Word of Christ to dwell in us richly and the Mind of Christ to govern our actions and attitudes.; our thoughts, and our motives. Paul knew that the most effective cure for a loss of peace and a lack of joy is a mind that is focused on Christ, a mind that is submissive to the leading and guidance of the Holy Spirit and a humble mind that seeks to esteem others as more important than themselves. When the mind of Christ is in us, our words and deeds, actions and attitudes will be a true reflection of our Saviour, Jesus Christ.

Confession: I have the mind of Christ. I will allow it to flow out so that people will see Christ through me.

April 19

1 Samuel 27-29; Luke 17:1-19

As he is

1 John 4:17
Love has been perfected among us in this: that we may have boldness in the day of judgment; because as He is, so are we in this world.

"God is love, and the one who abides in love abides in God, and God abides in him." By abiding in God and His love, love is perfected in us. The result of this perfected love is that we will have confidence in the day of judgment. The basis for this confidence is our conformity to the character of Jesus Christ. The test of whether we truly love God is our love for one another. In 1Jn 4:12, John declared that God lives in us if we love each other, and His love is made complete in us. Our walk with God should be a daily experience of getting to know Him better and better, for as He is, so are we in this world.

Confession: Lord, let people see Jesus in me. Let Your love flow through me.

April 20

1 Samuel 30-31; Luke 17:20-37

Who is your friend

Proverbs 13:20
He who walks with wise men will be wise, But the companion of fools will be destroyed.

Who we surround ourselves with most will significantly affect us negatively or positively. Whoever walks with the wise becomes wise. We want to walk alongside intelligent people. The wisdom the Bible is talking about here is not the wisdom according to the world. This is wisdom according to God and His word. Remember, the beginning of wisdom is the fear of God. So, we want to walk with people who fear God. We want to be around people who reverence God, who follow and worship God, and who obey God's word and try to liveaccording to it by God's grace.

Confession: Lord, help me to choose my friends wisely.

April 21

2 Samuel 1-3; Luke 18:1-17

Ingredient for fruitfulness

2 Peter 1:5-8
But also for this very reason, giving all diligence, add to your faith virtue, to virtue knowledge, to knowledge self-control, to self-control perseverance, to perseverance godliness, to godliness brotherly kindness, and to brotherly kindness love. For if these things are yours and abound, you will be neither barren nor unfruitful in the knowledge of our Lord Jesus Christ.

"If these things are in you, "This is not a list of imperatives, duties, or activities. Peter is not writing about "how-to," but about the kind of person, the Christian should strive to become. These character qualities he listed in the scripture above are the particular character qualities of God that should also be evident in our lives. These qualities will help us increase in the knowledge of our Lord Jesus Christ. We need to add these character qualities to our faith on purpose.

Confession: I will be diligent in adding these character qualities to my faith with the help of the Holy Spirit.

April 22

2 Samuel 4-6; Luke 18:18-43

How to please God

Hebrews 11:6
But without faith it is impossible to please Him, for he who comes to God must believe that He is, and that He is a rewarder of those who diligently seek Him.

Once we have believed in God's saving grace through faith in Christ, we are also to believe that "He rewards those that seek Him," as stated in the Scripture above. There is rejoicing in heaven when a sinner believes, but we genuinely please Him when we LIVE by faith. We please Him when life's difficult circumstances are not influencing us. If we desire to please our Heavenly Father, we must live by faith and not by sight. Our Christian life is a journey of faith, and it pleases God. When God is pleased, He turns everything around for our good. Faith sees the invisible.

Confession: Lord, I receive grace to please You by walking in faith.

April 23

2 Samuel 7-9; Luke 19:1-28

Accept one another

Colossians 3:13
bearing with one another, and forgiving one another, if anyone has a complaint against another; even as Christ forgave you, so you also must do.

Forbearing with one another describes patiently enduring the faults and failings of others in a kind, gracious, and godly manner. It is putting up with our brothers and sisters' inevitable misbehaviour and fluctuating attitudes with a spirit of gentleness, grace, understanding, patience, and endurance. The greatest of all incentives towards Godly forgiveness of others is rooted in the truth that God forgave us freely and forever. He forgave our sin - past, present, and future, for Christ's sake. He forgave each one of us of all our wrongdoings, and we, in turn, are to follow His godly example. Unforgiveness is an open door for the devil to come in and steal.

Confession: I receive grace to forgive people in Jesus' name.

April 24

2 Samuel 10-12; Luke 19:29-48

A man's heart

Proverbs 27:19
As in water face reflects face, So a man's heart reveals the man.

Man's countenance is frequently an index of his thoughts, and the condition of his mind is often displayed in his words, ways, will, and walk. As a man thinks, so is he. Whatever becomes the central focus of that man's mind influences his heart and is displayed in the outworking of his life. The Word of God is the truthful mirror into which we should look carefully. The Bible is the still water-pool in which to gaze day by day, for the face of Christ is the reflection upon which our hearts should rest. May we all with unveiled faces, gaze at the glory of the Lord as beholding HIM in the mirror, so that we may be transformed into His glorious image, from glory to glory - through the power of the indwelling Spirit of the Lord.

Confession: Help me, Lord, to renew my mind daily through Your word.

April 25

2 Samuel 13-14; Luke 20:1-26

Remember lot's wife

Luke 17:32
Remember Lot's wife.

In speaking to His disciples about a coming time of great destruction, Jesus mentioned what happened to Lot's wife and the destruction of Sodom and Gomorrah. "Remember Lot's wife. "Lot's wife lost her life because she "looked back." This was more than just a glance over the shoulder; it was a look of longing that indicated reluctance to leave or a desire to return. Whatever the case, the point is, that she was called to desert everything to save her life, but she could not let go, and she paid for it with her life. In Judaism, Lot's wife became a symbol of a rebellious unbeliever. In context, Jesus is talking about people who want to follow Him but are hindered by their concern for other things. It is not just that they look back, but they have divided loyalties, like Lot's wife.

Confession: Help me, Lord, to be loyal to You at all times.

April 26

2 Samuel 15-16; Luke 20:27-47

Whatever a man sows

Galatians 6:7
Do not be deceived, God is not mocked; for whatever a man sows, that he will also reap.

God set a principle of sowing and reaping, such that each of us reap a harvest of what we sow. Whatever we choose to plant in our lives, whether for good or evil, will bring forth the fruit of that choice. Many are suffering today because of the evil seed sown into their lives. May we learn the lesson of sowing and reaping, and may we do all things to the glory of God. It's a matter of time. The seed will produce fruit, either good or bad. The Lord will not allow His name to be disdained or trifled with, by those that ignore His Word and His will or by those that set aside His precepts and principles. Treat people as you would want to be treated.

Confession: I will sow seeds of righteousness in Jesus' name.

April 27

2 Samuel 17-18; Luke 21:1-19

Passions and desires

Galatians 5:24
And those who are Christ's have crucified the flesh with its passions and desires.

The moment we are saved, we can live godly in Christ Jesus. The flesh, with all its passion and desires, is crucified. This does not mean that the sinful nature is eradicated or rendered inactive, but it does mean that we can live godly in Christ Jesus and develop the fruit of righteousness by grace through faith. The Holy Spirit is in us to help us. He strengthens us and gives us the power to overcome the flesh. We have victory in Christ Jesus. All we need to do is appropriate the new life in Christ, lay hold of what is already ours in Christ by faith.

Confession: Thank You, Lord, for the grace to live above the flesh.

April 28

2 Samuel 19-20; Luke 21:20-38

The handwritten

Colossians 2:14
having wiped out the handwriting of requirements that was against us, which was contrary to us. And He has taken it out of the way, having nailed it to the cross.

The Law demands death sentence for every man and every woman, but Jesus "wiped out the handwriting of requirements that was against us." He fulfilled the righteous requirement of the Law on our behalf and destroyed the demands of the law against us. The wonderful gospel of Christ addresses this issue forever, and all of our defects are cancelled by the blood of the Lamb. He became the complete sacrifice for both the sins we committed during our lifetime and the sinful nature we inherited in our very being. Don't let the devil deceive you by telling you that God is angry with you because of your past life. The blood of Jesus is speaking continually on your behalf.

Confession: Thank You, Lord, for wiping out the handwritten of the devil against us.

April 29

2 Samuel 21-22; Luke 22:1-30

I have not seen

Psalm 37:25
I have been young, and now am old, Yet I have not seen the righteous forsaken, Nor his descendants begging bread.

The children of the righteous who follow God's way and obey His word will not be forsaken. God will extend His blessing to the seed of the righteous. David has seen and experienced God's faithfulness. He believed that God would provide for him always. No matter how difficult the crisis we may face, life can never create a vacuum or void that God cannot fill. There are times when our humanity perceives the lateness of the hour as the failure of God. However, God always smiles at our impatience with the knowledge that He can do more in a moment than man can do in a millennium. That is why the power of God to provide cannot be measured by time but only by trust.

Confession: Thank You, Father, for supplying all my needs.

April 30

2 Samuel 23-24; Luke 22:31-53

By their fruits

Matthew 7:16
You will know them by their fruits. Do men gather grapes from thornbushes or figs from thistles?

Jesus says, "You will know them by their fruit," what does "fruit" mean? Jesus gave the illustration of grapevines and fig trees. When we see grapevines, we expect them to contain grapes in season. We also expect fig trees to produce figs. Every word and every action is fruit from our hearts. We can only bring good fruit if our heart is renewed with the word of God daily. Sinners sin because that's what is in their hearts. Thieves steal, rapists rape and adulterers cheat because those sins are the fruit being produced from an evil heart. "You will know them by their fruit." No matter how good or convincing someone sounds, his message should be avoided if he bears bad fruit.

Confession: Lord, help me to bear good fruit for Your glory.

May 1

1 Kings 1-2; Luke 22:54-71

The snare is broken

Psalm 124:7
Our soul has escaped as a bird from the snare of the fowlers; The snare is broken, and we have escaped.

We seemed to be caught by the enemy. He appeared to have us entirely in his power. But escape came to us as it does to the bird when it finds the net suddenly broken, and he could escape easily. Just as the bird could not get out of the snare, so the soul cannot escape from eternal death. But God has made a way of escape through the death of Jesus Christ. There is freedom in Christ Jesus. Hear this, ye that are slaves to drunkenness, drugs, depression, lust or any addiction whatsoever, God can deliver you. The blood of Jesus can set you free if you believe in His saving grace. Whatever problem you are trapped in, the gracious hand that once was nailed to the cross can set you free.

Confession: Thank You, Father, for making a way of escape for us.

May 2

1 Kings 3-5; Luke 23:1-26

A word in season

Isaiah 50:4
"The Lord God has given Me The tongue of the learned, That I should know how to speak A word in season to him who is weary. He awakens Me morning by morning, He awakens My ear To hear as the learned.

This is a call for us as Christians to be a light to the world. It's about being conscious of our assignment in this world. We are to sustain the weary ones with a word of encouragement. How can we achieve this if we are tired and discouraged by life's challenges? Where then can the weary run to? We are the light of the world, and we cannot be hidden. We should be a channel of blessing to someone every day, put a smile on someone's face, give a word of comfort and bring hope to the hopeless. We are to draw our strength from God daily.

Confession: Lord, make me a channel of blessing to someone today in Jesus' name.

May 3

1 Kings 6-7; Luke 23:27-38

Grow in grace

2 Peter 3:18
But grow in grace, and in the knowledge of our Lord and Saviour Jesus Christ. To him be glory both now and forever. Amen.

Spiritual growth is an ongoing process of becoming more like the Lord Jesus. More grace is added to the grace we have already received as we mature in faith and change into the beautiful image and likeness of the Lord Jesus. Just as we need physical exercise and nourishing food for our bodies to grow and develop, we also need spiritual exercise and nutrition to mature in faith. We need the milk and meat of the Word of God to become strong in the Lord, so that we can carry out the work God has prepared for us. Growing in God's grace is not the accumulation of facts and information about the Lord Jesus but a day-by-day transformation of our life. As we look into the word of God, we become increasingly like Him in disposition and character.

Confession: Help me, Lord, to grow in grace and knowledge of our Lord Jesus Christ.

May 4

1 Kings 8-9; Luke 23:39-56

The golden rule

Matthew 7: 12
Therefore all things whatsoever ye would that men should do to you, do ye even so to them: for this is the law and the prophets.

This verse is a guiding principle for Christians and should influence our attitudes, motives and actions. It should be a life principle that impacts every area of our lives. We need to practice this principle with everyone we meet daily. The scripture above is called The "golden rule". It is an attitude of the life of a spirit-filled Christian. It should be evident in the life of any believer who is learning to walk in spirit and truth. "The golden rule" is the guiding principle of the man or woman who is growing in grace and learning to love as Christ loved us and gave Himself for us.

Confession: I will treat people the way I want to be treated.

May 5

1 Kings 10-11; Luke 24:1-35

If you return

Job 22:23
If you return to the Almighty, you will be built up; You will remove iniquity far from your tents.

God's divine restoration touches the sinner's nature when he repents and returns to God. Many of God's children are not enjoying the blessing of God because they have soiled their hands with iniquity. They have opened the door for the enemy through their sinful ways. Some live in fornication, adultery, lies, and other sinful attitudes. They are not faithful to God's ways. But God's hands are wide open to receive anyone who will confess and forsake his wicked ways. God will lift him from the dust and set him on his feet again. God cannot behold iniquity, but He is faithful and just to forgive us when we repent. Thus the restored person is made a temple for the indwelling of the Holy Ghost, who is a fortress and present help in time of need. We can call upon Him for help anytime.

Confession: Lord, I return to you. Help me to keep iniquity far from me.

May 6

1 Kings 12-13; Luke 24:36-53

The mystery of God

Colossians 2:2
that their hearts may be encouraged, being knit together in love, and attaining to all riches of the full assurance of understanding, to the knowledge of the mystery of God, both of the Father and of Christ,

Paul's stated purpose in this verse should be the motivation for all of God's children in these increasingly evil days in which we are living so that in Christ we may encourage one another in the faith and be united together in Godly love of the truth. This shows that unity among believers will enhance spiritual growth and cause revival to flow in our midst continually. Apostle Paul here prays for our hearts to be encouraged and be knitted together in love. This is a powerful prayer point; we should pray individually and collectively as a church. The effect of this is that we will gain access to the mystery of God, which is Christ.

Confession: Lord, may our hearts be encouraged as we walk in love.

May 7

1 Kings 14-15; John 1:1-28

Let your ways please God

Proverbs 16:7
When a man's ways please the Lord, He makes even his enemies to be at peace with him.

The question before all of us today is, "who do we or who is it that we are striving to please the most in our life? Is it your spouse, family, children, boss, or yourself? Or Is it God? We are reminded in scripture today that the only way to have true "peace" with our enemies is to live our lives in a way that pleases God and not man. People of God, keep this in mind. Pleasing God does not mean that you won't have enemies because Jesus had them too. But, what it does mean is that God will cause them to be at peace with you because you are following the word of God, walking in love and trusting Him in all things. He will fight for you and cause your enemies to be at peace with you.

Confession: Lord, I receive the grace to please You in my walk of faith and love.

May 8

1 Kings 16-18; John 1:29-51

We wrestle

Ephesians 6:12
For we do not wrestle against flesh and blood, but against principalities, against powers, against the rulers of the darkness of this age, against spiritual hosts of wickedness in the heavenly places.

Our battle is not against flesh and blood but against spiritual wickedness, against the spirit that now works in the sons of disobedience. It is the Holy Spirit of God, Who works in believers. But the spirit of wickedness works in the sons of disobedience. We are in Christ, and He is in us. We are to fight this enemy with spiritual weapons that God has provided through his Word and prayer. In verse 17 of Ephesians 6, we are told to take the sword of the Spirit, which is the word of God. You need to know the right word of God to use in different challenges that confront you. The more you speak the right word in prayer, the deeper the sword of God's word goes deep to the root of the issue and will eventually prevail (Acts 19:20).

Confession: The word of God I am speaking over my life will prevail in Jesus name.

May 9

1 Kings 19-20; John 2

The overcomers' weapon

Revelation 12:11
And they overcame him by the blood of the Lamb and by the word of their testimony, and they did not love their lives to the death.

The foundational bedrock upon which all victory rests is in the shed blood of Christ - the Lamb that was slain - the perfect Sacrifice, Who with one glorious cry of, "IT IS FINISHED," pronounced sin, death, and hell, 'forever conquered'. Nothing can dislodge that unshakably firm foundation. We need to testify about our victory in Christ Jesus, declaring what the word of God said about our situation. They overcame sickness, barrenness, addiction, depression, oppression, and affliction of all kinds by the blood of the lamb and the word of their testimony. When you understand that life and death are in the power of the tongue (proverb 18:21), you will consciously declare the word of God on purpose.

Confession: I will declare the word of God on purpose every they.

May 10

1 Kings 21-22; John 3:1-21

The devil will flee

James 4:7
Therefore submit to God. Resist the devil, and he will flee from you.

This is an appeal from Apostle James to us as believers. We are to resist the devil, and he will flee from us. In order to overcome the temptations, we are instructed to resist: to resist the devil, to resist the temptation, to resist the sin, but before resisting, we need to submit to God, to His word, to His ways and instructions. Our obedience has to be complete, then we can have boldness to resist the devil, and he has no choice but to obey and flee. When the devil is not obeying, you need to check your submission to God. Are you living in total obedience to God and following His precepts daily?

Confession: I will submit to God and resist the world's influences, the flesh and the devil in Jesus' name.

May 11

2 Kings 1-3; John 3:22-36

Compassion

Matthew 14:14
And Jesus went forth, and saw a great multitude, and was moved with compassion toward them, and he healed their sick.

Compassion is a deeper kind of empathy, one that is not content to sit at the margins and merely observe the pain of others. Compassion cannot sit by; it heals, moves toward those suffering, and puts itself at risk on behalf of others. Look again at Jesus' examples in the scripture above. He forsakes His reputation, offending the sensibilities of the religious leaders. Jesus's compassion leads Him to heal the sick, raise the dead, and bless sinners with His presence. Anywhere he shows up, darkness flees. As ambassadors of Christ, we are to bring light where there is darkness, for we are the light of the world. We cannot be relevant to the world if there is no darkness.

Confession: I am the light of the world. I bring light where there is darkness.

May 12

2 Kings 4-5; John 4:1-30

You will see the Lord

Hebrews 12:14
Pursue peace with all people, and holiness, without which no one will see the Lord

"Seeing the Lord" is our ultimate goal. This is what we all want, what we all genuinely desire, consciously and unconsciously. But the scriptures say we need first to learn how to live peaceably with all men through the knowledge of God's word, and then holiness is required. God is Holy, and nothing unholy can abide in His presence. Holiness is the manifest nature of God. The day we ask Christ to come into our hearts, the first thing that Christ's arrival brings into our hearts is the Holiness of His Father. However, this holiness must also become our lifestyle, and this is possible through the Holy Spirit who also came with Christ into our hearts, not only to cleanse our hearts from the guilt of sin but also to gives us the power to turn away from sin and live in obedient to the word of God. Christ and the Holy Spirit make the difference that people see daily in every true believer.

Confession: I will pursue peace with all men and holiness. I will see the Lord in Jesus name.

May 13

2 Kings 6-8; John 4:31-54

Do not touch

Psalm 105:14-15
He permitted no one to do them wrong; Yes, He rebuked kings for their sakes,
Saying, "Do not touch My anointed ones, And do My prophets no harm."

This brief verse contains a powerful warning from the Lord. And He meant every word of it. As believers, we all are God's anointed one. When God issued His warning, He gave the warning to everyone living on earth: He said, "I chose these people to be My portion. And I anointed them to be separated unto Me. From that time forward, I have never allowed any person or nation to do them harm." God is fighting for us even when we cannot see it physically. But as Christians, we must be careful of speaking against the anointed men of God. Even when they make mistakes, we should pray for them and allow God to chastise them. Remember what happened to Aaron and Miriam When They murmured against Moses. Numbers 12:1-15.

Confession: I am the Lord anointed; I am untouchable.

May 14

2 Kings 9-11; John 5:1-24

One thing is needful

Luke 10:41-42
And Jesus answered and said to her, "Martha, Martha, you are worried and troubled about many things. But one thing is needed, and Mary has chosen that good part, which will not be taken away from her."

Unless we sit at His feet and spend quality time communing with our Lord: our life will be fruitless, our work will become tedious, and our witness will be void of power. Mary gave her time to one thing that is needful. She liked sitting at the feet of the Lord Jesus communing with her Saviour, listening to His word, looking to Him, learning of Him, loving to be with Him, and pouring out her worship to Him, and in so doing, her spirit was refreshed, and her soul revived. Many of us, like Martha, are worried and troubled about many things. We neglect the most important thing, which is the presence of the Lord. There is healing, deliverance and peace in His presence. God will bring peace to every trouble as you surrender all to Him in prayer.

Confession: I have chosen the good part by regularly communing with the Lord.

May 15

2 Kings 12-14; John 5:25-47

Inside out

Romans 8:1

There is therefore now no condemnation to those who are in Christ Jesus, who do not walk according to the flesh, but according to the Spirit.

The wrath of God was poured out upon the Lord Jesus Christ at Calvary in payment for the sin of the whole world so that those that believe would not be placed under condemnation. Therefore, there is now no condemnation for those in union with Jesus, who also walk according to the spirit. Those who are not ruled by the flesh but obey the voice of the Holy Spirit will become more like Jesus every day. Paul encourages us that we do not need to fear condemnation because we can come to God as our loving, forgiving Father (Romans 8:15–16). Christians who live in shame and guilt over past failures are needlessly condemning themselves when they ought to be "forgetting what is behind and straining toward what is ahead" (Philippians 3:13).

Confession: Thank You, heavenly Father, that there is no condemnation for those who are in Christ Jesus.

May 16

2 Kings 15-17; John 6:1-21

The word of God is life

Matthew 6:63
It is the spirit that quickeneth; the flesh profiteth nothing: the words that I speak unto you, they are spirit, and they are life.

The word of God is living, and it is spiritual. It has the ability to give life to any adverse situation. The word of God is powerful (Hebrews 4:12). It is full of healing virtues. We are encouraged to attend to God's word in proverb 4:20-22; the scripture says that the word of God is life to those who find them. The fact is that God has spoken *from* the very conception of creation, and He still speaks today to any and all who will listen. It is in the nature of God to speak, to reveal His will. If we want to get close to God, we must develop a continuous habit of meditating and speaking the word of God until we get to the place of full persuasion. This happens when there is an entrance that brings understanding.

Confession: I will meditate on God’s word continually.

May 17

2 Kings 18-19; John 6:22-44

Come see a man

John 4:28-29

The woman then left her waterpot, went her way into the city, and said to the men, "Come, see a Man who told me all things that I ever did. Could this be the Christ?"

This woman was desperate, hopeless and in despair. When she met Jesus, Jesus told her all about everything she had done in her life. He was specific in even telling her that He knew she had been married five times and that the man she is with now is not her husband. Jesus did not tell her about her past as a means of belittling her, but to make her aware that the hope that she had been in pursuit of is right there before her. Hope is what Jesus offers every day at no cost to you and I, for He has paid our debt so we can have abundant life. This woman became an evangelist when she realized that she had met the one who could satisfy her inner thirst and give her hope and encouragement.

Confession: Thank you, Jesus. You are the answer for the world today.

May 18

2 Kings 20-22; John 6:45-71

Put on the new man

Colossians 3:9-10
Do not lie to one another, since you have put off the old man with his deeds, and have put on the new man who is renewed in knowledge according to the image of Him who created him.

To "Put on" the new man is like putting on fresh, clean clothes after removing dirty ones. Have you put away that old man? The old man is full of sin and worldliness. The new man is the one who is full of the righteousness and holiness of God. The only way to put off the old man is to strengthen the new man. This you can do through diligent study of God's word and meditation. The sword of the Spirit is the word of God. As believers, we must put on the new man daily. The fruit of the renewed man is love, joy, peace, longsuffering, and faith (Galatians 5:22-23). As we behold Christ through His word continually, we are renewed and become Christ-like to which we are called.

Confession: I receive the grace to put on the new man daily.

May 19

2 Kings 23-25; John 7:1-31

The will of God

1 John 2:17
And the world is passing away, and the lust of it; but he who does the will of God abides forever.

The world indeed is passing away and those sensational things of the flesh. But it will one day be replaced with a new heaven and a new earth, which should become our prime viewpoint. The lust of the flesh and the pride of life are futile and false, but the word of God will last forever. “He who does the will of God shallabide forever”. The word of God is the revealed will of God, and many of God’s children who are doers of the word and are obedient to the voice of the Holy Spirit will abide forever. Are you one of them? Many are just attending gatherings of believers, but they are not putting the word of God into practice.

Confession: Lord, help me to be a doer of Your word and to obey the voice of the Holy Spirit.

May 20

1 Chronicles 1-2; John 7:32-53

Power to declare

Job 22:28
You will also declare a thing, And it will be established for you; So light will shine on your ways.

The scripture above states that you will declare a thing, and it will be established; light will shine on your way. It means that nothing will be established without the utterance of God's word. The whole earth was in darkness until the Lord uttered His word. The earth was void, darkness was upon the face of the water, and God said: "Let there be light." He created something out of nothing. You, too, can issue decrees today, and something will happen in your life. The word of God says: If any of you shall say to the mountain: Be thou removed and cast into the sea and shall not doubt in his heart, but shall believe that those things which he said shall come to pass; he shall have whatever he saith (Matthew 11:23). You can rise in faith and declare the word standing on the promises of God.

Confession: Thank you, Father, for the power to declare your word. Your light shall shine on our ways as we declare them in Jesus name.

May 21

1 Chronicles 3-5; John 8:1-20

Share all good things

Galatians 6:6
Let him that is taught in the word communicate unto him that teacheth in all good things.

Who is “anyone”? It is the congregation of a body of believers. Who is the “instructor”? Anyone who has devoted their life to instructing the church in the word of God. What are the “good things”? They are the good things, God’s blessings which He freely pours out on his people, from the skills and talents that He gives them, and the encouragements they receive from day to day, to all the financial or material blessings that God sees fit to entrust to His people. God expects us to use our talents for His glory and give our material blessings to support the work of God. Sowing and reaping blessings in this way is a biblical principle that benefits both the giver and the one that receives – as well as honouring the Lord our God, from whom all blessings flow.

Confession: I will share all good things with my instructors and the body of Christ.

May 22

1 Chronicles 6-7; John 8:21-36

It is unconditional

Matthew 5:44-45
But I say to you, love your enemies, bless those who curse you, do good to those who hate you, and pray for those who spitefully use you and persecute you, that you may be sons of your Father in heaven; for He makes His sun rise on the evil and the good, and sends rain on the just and the unjust.

Our Father in Heaven loves all of His children, those who love Him and honour Him by keeping His commandments, as well as those who reject Him. He allows the sun to shine and the rain to fall on all of His children. Both obedient and disobedient, and He knows that all of His children will react in different ways, some positively and some negatively. But regardless of what we do, He will continue to love us and have hope for us. By teaching these words in the Sermon on the Mount, Jesus is telling us that our Heavenly Father wants us to develop that same kind of love that He has for the entire family of humanity. He wants us to love those who love us and those who hate us.

Confession: Lord, I receive the grace to walk in love towards everyone.

May 23

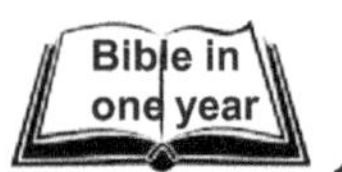

1 Chronicles 8-10; John 8:37-59

I am wiser

Psalm 119:98
Thou through thy commandments hast made me wiser than mine enemies: for they are ever with me.

How can you be wiser than your enemies? By simply trusting and walking in the light of God's word. The devil cannot stand your faith. To maintain a faith-filled life is wisdom. It is impossible to be wise apart from living a life of confidence in the Son of God. The law of the Lord teaches us the way of wisdom and how to deal wisely with the affairs of life. The greatest treasure of practical knowledge is found in the sublime commandment given by our Lord Jesus Himself: "Repent and believe in the gospel" (Mark 1:15). That divine edict contains the key to all the wisdom anyone could ever dream of in a thousand lifetimes. The fear of the Lord is the beginning of wisdom.

Confession: I will hold on to the word of God. For there lies the wisdom for life.

May 24

1 Chronicles 11-13; John 9:1-23

They that wait for him

Lamentations 3:25-26
The Lord is good to those who wait for Him, To the soul who seeks Him. It is good that one should hope and wait quietly For the salvation of the Lord.

There is something good here. What is it? To wait on the Lord. This means to place your hope in Him, to trust that God is the one Who can deliver you. But why is waiting so difficult? Because it feels as if we're not doing anything. And that's the point. You're not doing anything, but the scripture above says that it is good that one waits quietly for God. Waiting is one of the greatest applications of the Christian faith. You are trusting God, placing your hope in Him, and expressing confidence that He is in control. When you can say, "Though he tarries," I will wait for him. This is "active patience". That season is when God will shape and define us the most.

Confession: I will wait on the Lord. He can perfect all that concerns me.

May 25

1 Chronicles 11-13; John 9:1-23

The blessed

Galatians 3:9
So then they which be of faith are blessed with faithful Abraham.

The scriptures preached the gospel beforehand when God made the promise to Abraham in Genesis 12:3 “In you shall all the nations be blessed.” God offered a solution before we understood we had a problem. From the very beginning, God intended that all people, including the Gentiles, would be saved through the same means: hearing with faith. So those of faith are blessed along with Abraham, who was the man of faith (3:9). Are you of faith? Do you believe in Jesus? Then you are " blessed. It’s s just a matter of time before the fruit will be visible if you continue to water your seed by fixing your eyes on Jesus, the Author and Finisher of your faith.

Confession: I am of faith and am blessed. Abraham's blessings are mine.

May 26

1 Chronicles 11-13; John 9:1-2

The man who trusts in the Lord

Jeremiah 17:7-8

"Blessed is the man who trusts in the Lord, And whose hope is the Lord. For he shall be like a tree planted by the waters, Which spreads out its roots by the river, And will not fear when heat comes; But its leaf will be green, And will not be anxious in the year of drought, Nor will cease from yielding fruit.

It pleases the very heart of God when His children depend on Him utterly, believe in His Word, and trust in His Son for salvation, for without having faith in who He is and what He had said, it is impossible to please Him. Without faith, we are ships without a rudder that are tossed and adrift on the merciless sea of life, for the one who draws near to God must believe that He exists and that He is a rewarder of those who diligently seek Him. Trusting in God and hoping in the Lord is to believe the reality of all He has disclosed to us in His Word. The man who does this will not be anxious but will yield fruit continually.

Confession: I am like a tree planted by the waters. I will not be anxious.

May 27

1 Chronicles 14-16; John 9:24-41

Rich in mercy

Ephesians 2:4-5
But God, who is rich in mercy, because of His great love with which He loved us, even when we were dead in trespasses, made us alive together with Christ (by grace you have been saved)

"By grace, you have been saved". It is because of the immeasurable length, eternal breadth, incalculable height and abundant depth of God's love that He demonstrated His love towards us by means of His grace and mercy. For He sent His only begotten Son to die for us so that we might live eternally. God did what He did out of His compassion and His love. We need to remember that this love for us was not based on who we were, what we had done, or how good of people we had become. God does not love us because we are lovable. There was nothing sweet about us, our sin was detestable in the eyes of God, but He loved us anyway.

Confession: Thank you, Lord, for Your unconditional love.

May 28

1 Chronicles 17-19; John 10:1-21

Favour is from God

Proverbs 12:2
A good man obtaineth favour of the Lord : but a man of wicked devices will he condemn.

A good man obeys God's instructions. A good man performs his work "heartily, as unto the Lord and not for men" (Colossians 3:23). Because of his service and faithfulness to the Lord, he will be rewarded by God. A good man finds favour with God because he lays hold of wisdom in the word of God and obeys them (Pr 8:35). A foolish man rejects wisdom and, by doing so, wrongs his soul and chooses death instead (Pr. 8:36). The defining difference between the two persons is how they treat wisdom, God's instructions for living found in the Bible. Are you a good man?

Confession: Help me, Lord, to walk in the light of Your word every day.

May 29

1 Chronicles 20-22; John 10:22-42

Good stewards

1 Peter 4:10
As each one has received a gift, minister it to one another, as good stewards of the manifold grace of God.

Christians are given spiritual gifts to fulfill a special function within the body of Christ. Each of us receives at least one spiritual gift, and Peter calls us to be good stewards of all we receive from the Lord. Our gift differs according to the grace God gives to each of us, and we are instructed to exercise them according to the proportion of faith we have received. Gifts are not for our selfish gratification but for the edification of the body of Christ. The grace that pours into our lives should become a channel of God's blessing, which in turn is poured out in service to others for His greater glory and praise. Are you using your gift to serve the Lord?

Confession: Thank you, Lord. I will use my gift for the edification of the body of Christ.

May 30

1 Chronicles 23; John 11:1-10

Serve Him with gladness

Psalm 100:2
Serve the Lord with gladness; Come before His presence with singing.

Uniting as one, in joyful psalms of rejoicing and lifting up our voices together in spiritual songs and harmonious hymns of praise, is the exciting theme that threads its way throughout the entire Bible. It was a song of rejoicing that moved the Lord to act on behalf of His people Israel, following the pleading prayer of King Jehoshaphat: For when they began singing and praising, the Lord set ambushes against the sons of Ammon, Moab, and Mount Seir, who had come against Judah – so they were routed. When you give God high praise, He is compelled to take over the battle. Praise is a warfare strategy that guarantees victory. You can celebrate the goodness of God in challenging times.

Confession: Thank you, Lord, Your praise shall continually be in my mouth.

May 31

1 Chronicles 24-25; John 11:11-17

Nothing shall offend them

Psalm 119:165
Great peace have they which love thy law: and nothing shall offend them.

"Great peace have they who love your law." Peace is a wonderful concept, and "great peace" is even better. Peace is man's highest hope and his fondest dream. There is a specific condition attached to the promise of great peace. This "great shalom" is given only to those who love God's law. We love this book because we love the One who wrote this book. His words have meaning for us because we know Him personally. Those who love the law are willing to obey the word of God in any situation. The second condition is, "Nothing shall offend them. Nothing will cause us to be angry or frustrated. But we will have a strong foundation in times of trouble.

Confession: I love the word of God. Nothing will offend me.

June 1

1 Chronicles 26-27; John 11:18-46

The valley shall be filled

Luke 3:5

Every valley shall be filled, and every mountain and hill shall be brought low; and the crooked shall be made straight, and the rough ways shall be made smooth;

This is a prophetic word to those who believe. "Every valley shall be filled, "meaning that all hindrances shall be taken out of the way: every mountain before you shall be brought low. Mountain of financial problems, marriage problems, and challenges of any kind. The Lord is stepping ahead of you into this new month.

You will see the salvation of the Lord. There shall be showers of blessing. The crooked places shall be straightened. All you need to do is prepare the way for the Lord by maintaining a worry-free heart. Let the joy of the Lord flood your heart as you give Him sacrificial praise; you will surely see the salvation of the Lord.

Confession: Thank you Father, I believe that I will see Your salvation.

June 2

Bible in one year

1 Chronicles 28-29; John 11:47-57

Light dominates darkness

John 1:5
And the light shineth in darkness; and the darkness comprehended it not.

When you believe in Jesus, not only do you leave the darkness and enter the light, you join the family of light. You become children of light. Paul said, "Once you were darkness, but now you are light in the Lord; walk as children of light" (Ephesians 5:8). The scripture above says, "The light shines in the darkness, and the darkness comprehended it not." The light will triumph. This means that Jesus will triumph through you, for He lives in you. We have been equipped for victory in every situation. It all depends on your approach to the challenges of life. We are the light of the world. When we appear, darkness flees because he cannot stand the light in us.

Confession: I am light; I will triumph in every situation in Jesus' name.

June 3

2 Chronicles 1-3; John 12:1-19

Amazing grace

Titus 2:11

For the grace of God that bringeth salvation hath appeared to all men,

In the passage above, Paul refers to the embodiment of grace in the person of Jesus Christ, who was "full of grace and truth" (John 1:14). Paul means that God's grace that appeared in the person of Christ offers salvation to all that hear of it "to all types of people, including those whom the world despises, even to slaves." No one is beyond the reach of God's grace. But the good news of God's grace is that no sinner is beyond the reach of God's grace. The apostle Paul was a persecutor of the church. He called himself the chief of sinners (1 Tim. 1:13, 15). But he experienced God's grace through the cross. If the chief of sinners found mercy, so can you! This is amazing grace. It saves us, and then it trains and motivates us to be godly people in this present age, zealous for good deeds, as we look for the appearing of the glory of our great God and Savior, Jesus Christ, who gave Himself for us.

Confession: Thank you, Father, for bringing salvation to all men.

June 4

2 Chronicles 4-6; John 12:20-50

The little foxes

Song of Solomon 2:15
Take us the foxes, the little foxes, that spoil the vines: for our vines have tender grapes.

What are the little foxes in our lives that gnaw away at the tender grapes of spiritual fruitfulness? These are the insidious little sins that are not easily seen. Lies, bitterness, anger, unforgiveness, fornication, adultery, malice, gossiping, a little concession to the world's standard. These "little foxes" are destructive, wreaking devastation like undetected cancer in our souls. We set spiritual laws in motion through words and action; when the consequences arise, we ask, "God, why me?" What about the little compromises with falsehood and error? Lies are unresolved in our Christian lives, even in some Christian marriages. These little foxes can hinder our growth and progress in life if we fail to deal with them.

Confession: Lord, I receive the grace to deal with the little foxes in my life in Jesus' name.

June 5

2 Chronicles 7-9; John 13:1-17

Sin defined

James 4:17
Therefore to him that knoweth to do good, and doeth it not, to him it is sin.

God has given us all we need for life and godliness. We have been given the Holy Scriptures, which provide clear teachings on living godly and walking in spirit and truth. In the scripture above, the apostle explains to us the consequences of knowing what is godly and honourable in the sight of the Lord and yet refusing to carry it out. Therefore, to the one who knows the right thing to do, he warns, yet does not do it – to him, it is a sin. As children of God, our whole life and attitude should be to live our life for Christ, every moment of the day, to present our lives as a living sacrifice to Him, to trust His word and walk in utter dependence on Him, moment by moment, for His greater glory.

Confession: Lord, I receive grace to do what is right always.

June 6

2 Chronicles 10-12; John 13:18-38

The broadway

Matthew 7:13
Enter ye in at the strait gate: for wide is the gate, and broad is the way, that leadeth to destruction, and many there be which go in thereat:

Jesus here shows us that there are two ways to travel through our Christian life. The spiritual gateway leads to an abundant and victorious life, a life of commitment to God, a life of obedience to His word. This is the straight gate, and the Lord encouraged us to enter through this gate as we travel through this world. But the one who chooses to live for self is the one who enters the broad way to destruction - losing their opportunity to die to self and to livefor Christ. Therefore, Broadway is identified as the road that most of the human race will take and is seen as the easy path that leads to destruction and the fires of hell. Which way do you choose?

Confession: I choose Your way Lord, a life of commitment to Your will.

June 7

2 Chronicles 13-16; John 14

Hidden treasures

Proverbs 2:1-2
My son, if thou wilt receive my words, and hide my commandments with thee; So that thou incline thine ear unto wisdom, and apply thine heart to understanding;

Here are two conditions to understand the fear of the LORD and find the knowledge and wisdom of God. These two traits separate wise men from foolish men; they separate godly men from profane men. "If thou wilt receive my words" is the first condition. Wisdom requires listening to the word of God. "If thou wilt hide my commandments with thee" is the second condition. Once you learn something, you must retain it. You must hide God's word in your heart by reviewing it enough to remember it. Then you can practice it because you speak and act from the abundance of the heart.

Confession: Lord, I receive grace to receive your word and retain it.

June 8

2 Chronicles 17-19; John 15

Who are your friends

Psalm 119:63
I am a companion of all them that fear thee, and of them that keep thy precepts.

Jesus said in the book of John 15:14: "You are my friends if you do whatever I command you." So: all who keep His commands are acknowledged by Him as His friends. The psalmist in the scripture says that he chose his associates and friends among those who worship God, not the profane and the wicked. "A man is known by the company that he keeps," and it is evidence of purity when we seek our companions and friends among the pious. It shows where the heart is, what the preferences are, the tastes, and the actual condition of the soul. A man may determine much about his character by asking himself what the character of his chosen friends is.

Confession: I will keep company with those who love God and keep His word.

June 9

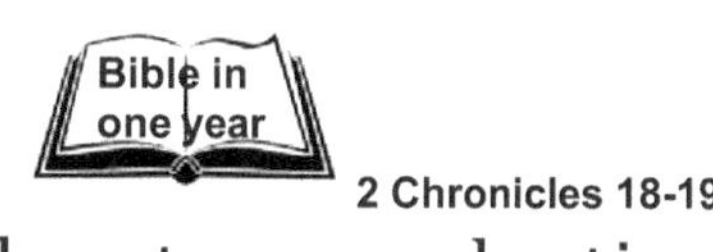

2 Chronicles 18-19

Work out your salvation

Philippians 2:12
Wherefore, my beloved, as ye have always obeyed, not as in my presence only, but now much more in my absence, work out your own salvation with fear and trembling.

We are told to work out our own salvation with "*fear and trembling*". This does not mean that we live our lives in panic and anxiety but with awe and reverence for God. It involves a sober assessment of yourself. Working out your salvation with fear and trembling means living with an intense desire to do what is right. Having received salvation as a gift, we must work zealously to live worthy of it. We must acknowledge that every sin is an offense against God and produces a sincere desire not to offend and grieve the Holy Spirit who is dwelling in us. The grace of God is available to us to obey, honor, please, and glorify Him in all things.

Confession: Thank you Lord for the gift of salvation, help me Lord to work out my own salvation in reverential fear.

June 10

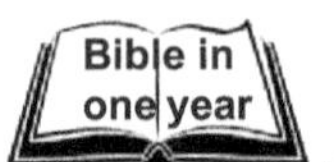

2 Chronicles 20-22; John 16:1-15

Your names are written

Luke 10:20
Notwithstanding in this rejoice not, that the spirits are subject unto you; but rather rejoice, because your names are written in heaven.

We came across the above passage in one of our family bible studies, and for the first time, I saw more reasons we should rejoice every day. The disciples were rejoicing because the powers of darkness were subject to them, but Jesus told them, rather rejoice because their names are written in heaven. Jesus points out that our joy should not be focused on the gifts, abilities, honour, and acclaim that God had graciously bestowed on us, but instead, we should rejoice that our names are written in the Book of Life. This should encourage us to maintain a joyful attitude as we await the coming of our Saviour Jesus Christ.

Confession: Thank You, Father, for my name, is written in the book of life.

June 11

2 Chronicles 23-25; John 16:16-33

Better things

Hebrews 12:24
And to Jesus the mediator of the new covenant, and to the blood of sprinkling, that speaketh better things than that of Abel.

The blood of Christ is infinitely superior to that of Abel, for Jesus offered His blood, which paid the price for the sins of the whole world, including your sins and mine. He was the Lamb of God, Who took away the sin of the world. And God is satisfied with Christ's sacrifice of Himself on account of all who live by faith. When we come to Christ by faith, we enter into the covenant of His blood. The blood of Jesus speaks mercy, pardon, victory, deliverance, and freedom. It says better things than that of Abel. Praise God that we are sprinkled with the precious blood of Jesus Christ, the one and only Mediator between God and man. You can rise in faith and plead the blood of Jesus against Satan. The blood of Jesus is our weapon of victory.

Confession: Thank you, Father, for the blood of Jesus that speaks better things for us.

June 12

2 Chronicles 26-28; John 17

It is for a while

1 Peter 5:10
But the God of all grace, who hath called us unto his eternal glory by Christ Jesus, after that ye have suffered a while, make you perfect, stablish, strengthen, settle you.

The Lord Jesus Himself learned obedience by the things He suffered, and after His time of suffering, Christ came into His eternal glory and willingly and joyfully shared it with all who trust in His name. Peter here reminds us that after we have experienced suffering for a little while, God in His grace will perfect, confirm, strengthen, and establish us. Despite the difficulties that would inevitably arise in our lives, we must understand that weeping may last for a night, but joy is sure to come in the morning. Suffering has lasting benefits for it establishes, strengthens, perfects, and matures the believer.

Confession: Help me, Lord, to walk worthy of You, not shrinking from the fiery trials of life, but that through them I will be firmly established in the faith.

June 13

2 Chronicles 29-31; John 18:1-23

A diligent man

Proverbs 22:29
Seest thou a man diligent in his business? he shall stand before kings; he shall not stand before mean men.

Diligence is a spiritual virtue. It is the key ingredient to success in life. It is the persistent, determined, constant, and earnest effort to complete a task. Until the spirit of diligence comes into play, excellence never becomes a reality. Being diligent requires work and focus. Even if you are told by a prophet that God said you would be very great, you must be diligent for it to be fulfilled. We must be desperate and hungry for the spirit of diligence. In one of our fasting and prayer times, the Lord told his servant pastor Ladejobi Elijah that to succeed in life, you need to put these four qualities to work: Desire, sleeplessness, education, and reproduction. Diligence is the keyword for all these qualities. Persistent effort in the area you are gifted with, will take you high.

Confession: I receive grace to be diligent in Jesus' name.

June 14

2 Chronicles 32-33; John 18:24-40

You are translated

Colossians 1:13
Who hath delivered us from the power of darkness, and hath translated us into the kingdom of his dear Son:

The kingdom of Satan is full of darkness and diseases, doom and destruction, desolation and death. But by a simple act of faith in Christ's finished work at Calvary, we have been lifted out of this shocking state of eternal slavery and transferred into Christ's glorious kingdom of everlasting light and life - the domain of God's only beloved Son. Now we can enjoy the peace of God, and deliverance fromoppression. We can enjoy divine fellowship with the Father. You have authority in the name of Jesus to claim your peace and freedom when the devil comes to steal it from you. You have the power to stop him. So, rise in faith and claim all the enemy has stolen from you.

Confession: I thank you, Father, for delivering me from the domain of darkness and transferring me into the kingdom of Your beloved Son.

June 15

2 Chronicles 34-36; John 19:1-22

As the days of a tree

Isaiah 65:22
They shall not build, and another inhabit; they shall not plant, and another eat: for as the days of a tree are the days of my people, and mine elect shall long enjoy the work of their hands.

"Mine elect shall long enjoy the work of their hands." Are you one of the elects, washed in the blood of the Lamb? Then this word of God is for you. We need to declare this word of God on purpose every day. We also need to get rid of things that shorten life: anxiety, sorrow, and lack of contentment. The Christian principles guard against these. The word of God encourages us to maintain a life of purity, temperance, serenity, and cheerfulness of spirit. These Christian principles are security for long-time enjoyment. Our part is to look unto Jesus, the Author and Finisher of our faith and be joyful always.

Confession: I shall long enjoy the work of my hands in Jesus' name.

June 16

Ezra 1-2; John 19:23-42

Be strong

2 Chronicles 15:7
Be ye strong therefore, and let not your hands be weak: for your work shall be rewarded.

We need to declare the above scripture repeatedly, speaking to ourselves with these encouraging words of God. Some situations may come the way that requires you to be strong, especially when you have other people looking up to you. You need to encourage yourself in the Lord and look unto God for a solution. Our strength comes from the Lord, so we need to deepen our fellowship with God. We need to spend more time in prayer, reading and meditating on the word of God. Remember, you can do all things through Christ who strengthens you. The scripture above says that our work shall be rewarded. Let's be encouraged by this and be strong to carry out God's assignment for us.

Confession: Thank you, Father, for making me strong and courageous.

June 17

Ezra 3-5; John 20

But his delight

Psalm 1:1-3

Blessed is the man that walketh not in the counsel of the ungodly, nor standeth in the way of sinners, nor sitteth in the seat of the scornful. But his delight is in the law of the Lord, and in his law doth he meditate day and night. And he shall be like a tree planted by the rivers of water, that bringeth forth his fruit in his season; his leaf also shall not wither; and whatsoever he doeth shall prosper.

The only way you will ever know what true happiness is and experience real blessings is to seek to become a "Psalm 1" man. This is the picture of the kind of men we should be. The description of Psalm 1 man begins with what he does not do. He will not walk through life following the counsel of the ungodly. This blessed man does not "stand in the way of sinners". He does not live in the same way as men who practice sin. This man derives pleasure from reading, studying and meditating on the word of God. The reward is that he will be like a tree planted by the rivers of water.

Confession: Help me, Lord, to be like the man described in Psalm 1.

June 18

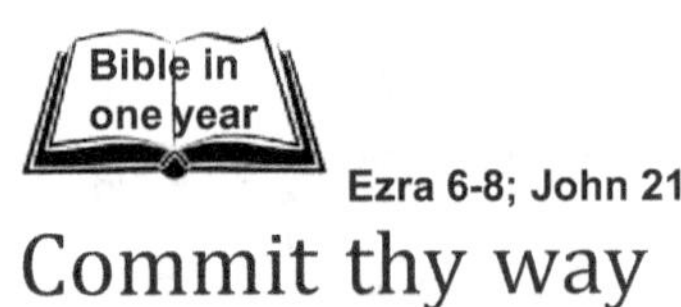

Ezra 6-8; John 21

Commit thy way

Psalm 37:5
Commit thy way unto the Lord; trust also in him; and he shall bring it to pass.

As Christians, if we commit all our ways to the Lord and trust God in everything, and believe all that He has told us in His Word, we would discover that our will would line up with God's will for our life. We are to trust God to carry out the ongoing work of sanctification in our lives so that we are conformed more and more into the image and likeness of Jesus Christ. Committing our way to the Lord means trusting Him to carry out all that He has promised to do in our lives. If we believe, we will stop fretting about all the happenings and problems in the world. We delight ourselves in the Lord by trusting His Word, resting in His promises, and committing everything into His hands. He can carry out His perfect will in each of our lives.

Confession: Lord, I commit all my ways into your hands. I believe you can perfect all that concerns me.

June 19

Ezra 9-10; Acts 1

You are anointed

2 Corinthians 1:21-22
Now he which stablisheth us with you in Christ, and hath anointed us, is God; Who hath also sealed us, and given the earnest of the Spirit in our hearts.

God calls us, saves us, sanctifies us, and anoints us. It is God who establishes us and brings us to spiritual maturity. Still, we need to cooperate with the Holy Spirit as we discipline ourselves and put the word of God into practice. We are not to remain in spiritual infancy. God wants us to grow spiritually and be established in the faith. But we see that many Christians are not producing fruit today because they are still babies after many years of being in the Lord. The truth is that there are many things God cannot commit into your hands if you decide to remain a baby. God is waiting for you to grow.

Confession: Thank you, Lord, for Your anointing. I receive grace to deepen my relationship with You.

June 20

Nehemiah 1-3; Acts 2:1-13

He will give life to your body

Romans 8:11
But if the Spirit of Him who raised Jesus from the dead dwells in you, He who raised Christ from the dead will also give life to your mortal bodies through His Spirit who dwells in you.

Our mortal bodies are tents that house our immortal spirit and eternal soul. They remain subject to death, sickness, and deceases. But the glorious truth in this verse is that we have hope in Christ - for the same Spirit that raised Him from the dead is dwelling in us as believers, giving life to our mortal bodies. The scripture above starts with, " But if the spirit of him who raised Christ from the dead dwells in you. " Have you asked Jesus to be your Lord and Saviour? If yes, the Holy Spirit is living in you. You can claim the healing of your mortal body because He who raised Christ from the dead is restoring life to every part of your body.

Confession: Thank you Father, I am healthy because Your Spirit supplies life to my mortal body.

June 21

Nehemiah 4-6; Acts 2:14-47

I will sing to the Lord

Psalm 13:5-6
But I have trusted in Your mercy; My heart shall rejoice in Your salvation. I will sing to the Lord, Because He has dealt bountifully with me.

Reading through this Psalm from the beginning, you will notice that David offers several rhetorical questions. How long will You forget me? How long will You hide Your face from me? David felt that the Lord had abandoned him. But feelings should never cloud the truth of God's word, for He has promised to be with us, even to the end of the age. Jesus, Himself warned us that we would have tribulation in this world. Paul added that all who live godly lives would suffer persecution. But Christ Himself encouraged us to be of good cheer, for I have overcome the world. In this verse above, David has finally realized the goodness of God even during life challenges and troubles. He said, "I will sing to the Lord." Have you decided to sing to the Lord regardless of the situation?

Confession: I have made up my mind to sing of your goodness forever.

June 22

Nehemiah 7-8; Acts 3

With favour

Psalm 5:12
For You, O Lord, will bless the righteous; With favour, You will surround him as with a shield.

When the favour of God is upon a man, he will be secured and protected against all oppositions. Favour will make help available for you at a time and from a place you least expected. Favour will single you out for the position you are not naturally qualified for, especially among others that are far better than you. The question is, "What opens the door for divine favour? The Bible testified about Noah in Genesis 6:9 that he was a just man. He was righteous and blameless in his generation, he was a worshiper, a man of faith, and he listened and obeyed God. I believe these qualities opened the door of favour for Noah to be chosen in his generation and for us all who are willing to walk with God.

Confession: Thank you, Father, for Your favour. I receive grace to keep the door of favour open in Jesus.

June 23

Nehemiah 9-11; Acts 4:1-22

They shall be filled

Matthew 5:6

Blessed are they which do hunger and thirst after righteousness: for they shall be filled.

Spiritual hunger is a good thing. It is the most excellent persuader for accomplishment. There is a spirit of desperation that accompanies spiritual hunger. One of the Holy Spirit's works is to create a hunger in our hearts for that event that God has promised. Daniel diligently set his face to pray about the deliverance of the children of Israel from their captivity in Babylon. The seventy years were fulfilled, but there was no deliverance until Daniel got so hungry that he fasted and prayed that the rescue might come. God's purpose comes to pass when the natural desire of God gets hold of us, and we pray fervently for it. If it becomes in your life the supreme cry, the paramount issue, when all the energies of your spirit, soul, and body are crying to God for the answer, it will come. Your hungry soul shall be filled.

Confession: Thank you, Father, I shall be filled as I cry out to You with all my heart.

June 24

Nehemiah 12-13; Acts 4:23-37

Long life

Psalm 91:16
With long life I will satisfy him, and show him My salvation."

With long life, will I satisfy him. God will satisfy His Children with long life as we desire, or until we are satisfied with life. A time will come when we will be "satisfied" with living when we will have no strong desire to remain on this earth. But desire to be with the Lord. Apostle Paul said in Philippians 1:23, "For I am hard-pressed between the two, having a desire to depart and be with Christ, *which is* far better." Yes, it is far better to be with Christ. When we finish our assignment here on earth, we will depart and be with the Lord. The promise extends beyond the grave: "Godliness is profitable unto all things, having promise of the life that now is, and of that which is to come." There is a glorious life awaiting the saints of God.

Confession: Thank you, Father, for the glorious life here now and a better life with You in eternity.

June 25

Esther 1-3; Acts 5:1-16

When a dumb donkey speaks

2 Peter 2:15-16

They have forsaken the right way and gone astray, following the way of Balaam the son of Beor, who loved the wages of unrighteousness; but he was rebuked for his iniquity: a dumb donkey speaking with a man's voice restrained the madness of the prophet.

Apostle Peter confirms the story of the talking donkey. He tells us that God used "The dumb donkey" to forbade the madness of the prophet. The donkey spoke to the prophet with a man's voice to restrain him from his evil ways. Had Balaam been faithful to God, refusing to be moved by his greed for riches, he would not have erred and eventually lost his path (Numbers 22-24). Many children of God have forsaken the right way, just like Balaam. They love the wages of unrighteousness. The right way is the way of the Lord. You, too, can choose the right way and allow the light of God to shine through you.

Confession: Lord, help me to choose the right way in all things.

June 26

Esther 4-6; Acts 5:17-42

Delight yourself in the Lord

Psalm 37:4
Delight thyself also in the LORD: and he shall give thee the desires of thine heart.

Taking delight in the Lord means that our hearts find peace and fulfilment in Him. The Scripture says He will give us the longings of our hearts. The idea behind this verse and others like it is that when we "delight" in the eternal things of God, our desires will begin to parallel His and we will never be unfulfilled. When we delight in Him, we take our sights off what we want and focus on what God desires. The best way to stop fretting is to take our eyes off the circumstances and fix them on Christ, who is the true source of a believer's delight. Many delights in wealth, status, material possessions, and other temporary things of this world, but they are never satisfied. Delighting in the Lord is a true treasure indeed: "Godliness with contentment is great gain.

Confession: I will delight myself in the Lord and trust him to perfect all that concerns me.

June 27

Esther 7-10; Acts 6

By the blood

Ephesians 2:13
But now in Christ Jesus you who once were far off have been brought near by the blood of Christ.

Before we were born-again into the family of God, we were without Christ, without heavenly citizenship, without a covenant relationship, without God's promises, without access to the throne of grace and hope in the world. We were godless sinners and members of a hopeless, sinful race. But now, through the blood of Christ, all restrictions in approaching our Creator have been lifted, and all barriers to our Father have been removed. We who were once dead are now made alive, hallelujah. Now in Christ Jesus - we who formerly were far off have been brought near by the blood of Christ. Don't let the devil deceive you about your past life. When you genuinely repent and ask God for forgiveness, God will forgive you, and He will remember it no more.

Confession: Thank You, father, we have freedom in Jesus' name.

June 28

Job 1-3; Acts 7:1-19

The work of our hands

Psalm 90:17
And let the beauty of the Lord our God be upon us, And establish the work of our hands for us; Yes, establish the work of our hands.

If the work of our hands will prosper and be established, it must come from God. The utmost we can do is accomplish the outward conditions of success with excellence in whatever we are doing. It's God alone that will crown our efforts with success both in our occupation and vacation. When Christians do their jobs with excellence and accountability, in a distinctively Christian manner, they cannot help but have a profound effect on the world around them. We are to show a good example by doing things orderly. Do you go to work late? Do you carry out your duty the way it should be done? May the grace of God continue to rest upon us and may the beauty of the Lord Jesus be seen in us and through us as we submit to the leading and guiding of the Holy Spirit in our life, doing all our work with excellence.

Confession: Help me, Lord, to do everything with excellence.

June 29

Job 4-6; Acts 7:20-43

We are blessed

Ephesian 1:3
Blessed be the God and Father of our Lord Jesus Christ, who hath blessed us with all spiritual blessings in heavenly places in Christ:

You are blessed. It's a fact. God has blessed you. He has poured out every spiritual blessing on you because of His love. You are a carrier of God's blessing. You may look around you now and ask, "am I blessed"? Yes, you are because of who you are and your faith in the Lord Jesus Christ. You are a child of the highest Creator of the whole universe. It's just a matter of time. Your time of manifestation will come. All blessings come to us through Jesus Christ. We can do nothing without Him (John 15:5), but we have every spiritual blessing in Him. In Him "are hidden all the treasures of wisdom and knowledge" (Colossians 2:3). In him, you will find the knowledge and wisdom to handle the issues of life. The Holy Spirit will give you the ideas and insight you need in your Christian journey.

Confession: Thank you, Father, for blessing us with every spiritual blessing in heavenly places.

June 30

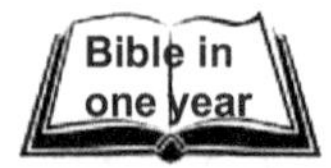

Job 7-9; Acts 7:44-60

Far from oppression

Isaiah 54:14
In righteousness you shall be established; You shall be far from oppression, for you shall not fear; And from terror, for it shall not come near you.

Righteousness means the ability to stand in the presence of the Father God without the sense of guilt or inferiority." Knowing your identity in Christ is crucial because it affects our relationship with God. Your prayer life is directly affected because of this. The more you walk in the consciousness of who you are in Christ, the more the activities of darkness will lose their power over your life. The bible says, "Even so Abraham believed God, and it was reckoned to him as righteousness." (Galatians 3:6). Abraham just believed in God, and God gave him righteousness. Do you believe in God and His promises? You need to walk in the consciousness of your right standing with God and refuse to fear because the Lord is with you.

Confession: I am established in righteousness. I am far from oppression.

July 1

Job 10-12; Acts 8:1-25

Fear not

Isaiah 52:12

For ye shall not go out with haste, nor go by flight: for the Lord will go before you; and the God of Israel will be your reward.

The Lord will go before you in this new month in Jesus name. God goes before us in battle. He prepares the way ahead of our arrival. But sometimes, God chooses to use the tactics of coming behind us. We need to stand still and see the salvation of the Lord. The account of this deliverance tactic was used when Moses was taking the Israelites out of the land of bondage, and they found themselves at the Red Sea. God had gone before them and forced Pharaoh to release them. However, now they needed God to stop the enemy behind. They moved forward in obedience to divine instruction, and God opened the path and came behind them and destroyed the army that followed them. God is waiting for your obedience.

Confession: Thank you, Father, for always going before and behind us.

July 2

Job 13-15; Acts 8:26-40

The greater one

1 John 4:4

Ye are of God, little children, and have overcome them: because greater is he that is in you, than he that is in the world.

The Spirit of God has taken up permanent residence in the hearts of all His children, and we have become the dwelling-place of the all-powerful, all-mighty, all-knowing, all-gracious God. Through His shed blood and bodily resurrection, Christ overcame. And through faith in Him, we also overcame by the BLOOD of the Lamb. We overcome because of the testimony of our faith in Him. We are overcomers because of what Christ has done on our account. The Greater One is in you, empowering you for victory in all circumstances, but you need to be bold and strong in the Lord. You need to see every challenge as an opportunity to stir up the lion in you, for Jesus is the lion of the tribe of Juda. Walking in the consciousness of the power of God in you will keep your faith strong to stand firm in every situation.

Confession: Thank you, Father. I have overcome because the Greater One is living in me.

July 3

Job 16-18; Acts 9:1-22

The oracle of God

1 Peter 4:11
If any man speak, let him speak as the oracles of God; if any man minister, let him do it as of the ability which God giveth: that God in all things may be glorified through Jesus Christ, to whom be praise and dominion for ever and ever. Amen.

The underlying emphasis in all that Peter says is that every facet of our lives must conform to the "oracles of God." Whether we speak, minister, or practice hospitality. All should be done to the glory of God. We must constantly be reminded of what God says. We must speak only as He has spoken to us. As parents, we must say what the word of God says about our children. As a child of God, you must speak as his oracle by confessing what God said in His word concerning you, your children, and your family. As ministers of God, we must hear from God and preach with practical service in the kingdom of God. May we be "stirred up" by "remembering" the sacred oracles as we endeavour to do just those things that will glorify and honour God.

Confession: Lord, I receive grace to speak as your oracle always.

July 4

Job 19-20; Acts 9:23-43

If the Lord wills

James 4:14-15
Whereas ye know not what shall be on the morrow. For what is your life? It is even a vapour, that appeareth for a little time, and then vanisheth away. For that ye ought to say, If the Lord will, we shall live, and do this, or that.

This teaches us that the activities and accomplishments of our lives are in God's hands. Not only are our lives in His hands, but our success is also in His hands. God governs what we accomplish daily, and we need to acknowledge him in all our plans and activities by consciously saying, If the Lord wills, I will do this or that, by the grace of God". This sentence should follow all our intentions as we daily trust him to perfect all that concerns us. Let us remember how wonderfully secure we are in the confidence that it is God who finally governs our lives.

Confession: Thank you Father, it is by your grace that I am alive today.

July 5

Job 21-22; Acts 10:1-23

Through Christ

Philippians 4:13
I can do all things through Christ which strengtheneth me.

It's a reminder, an encouragement, that though life may be tough, God is with you. We should encourage ourselves with this verse when life's challenges are pressing hard on us, trusting God in whatever life throws our way because God is with us.
Paul challenges us to view happiness through a different lens. All we need is Jesus. It's through him and him alone that we get our strength. We will fail whenever we lose sight of that and try to do things through our power. Paul was kept in the dark and damp prison cell with little food to eat. Yet he could write the scripture above; why? Because he had what matters most. Jesus is all we need. We need to be content in Jesus alone. Our joy should not only come from the things happening around us. The joy of the Lord should be our strength. We can do ALL things through Christ who strengthens us.

Confession: Thank you, Father, I can do all things through Christ who strengthens me.

July 6

Job 23-25; Acts 10:24-48

Fat and flourishing

Psalm 92:12-14
The righteous shall flourish like the palm tree: he shall grow like a cedar in Lebanon. Those that be planted in the house of the Lord shall flourish in the courts of our God. They shall still bring forth fruit in old age; they shall be fat and flourishing;

This promise is for those who have made the presence of God their dwelling place. Jesus Christ is the living Word of God, and in Him is life. Spiritual life comes through hearing the Word of God and having faith in His Word. As Christians, we must abide in the life-giving vine of Jesus and His Word to be fruitful. Grapes broken prematurely from thevine shrivel and die on the ground. The juice and fatness of the grape come only from their vine. The fruitfulness of Christians comes from their continuing connection to the vine, our Lord Jesus Christ and being filled with the life-giving power of His Word and Spirit. How much of your time do you give Him every day?

Confession: Help me, Lord, to remain in your presence so that I will continue to flourish.

July 7

Job 26-28; Acts 11

The flesh is weak

Matthew 26:41
Watch and pray, that ye enter not into temptation: the spirit indeed is willing, but the flesh is weak.

"The Spirit is willing, but the flesh is weak". The spirit is willing to preach the word, forgive, and walk-in love. To live in obedience to Gods word, but the flesh is weak. Jesus gave us the key to strengthening the spirit. There is no respite from the attacks of the enemy, for any child of God, and Christ's urgent warning to us as Christians is to watch and keep on watching, to pray and keep on praying. The spirit is willing, but the flesh is weak - but those that utterly depend on God, abide in Christ and pray in unity with the Holy Spirit are given the strength to overcome the world, the flesh, and the devil - for Christ not only paid the price for our sin but broke the power of sin in the lives of all who believe. Only as we submit to God in humble submission and watchful prayer we can resist the evil one.

Confession: I receive grace to watch and pray in Jesus' name.

July 8

Job 29-30; Acts 12

Power to tread

Luke 10:19

Behold, I give unto you power to tread on serpents and scorpions, and over all the power of the enemy: and nothing shall by any means hurt you.

In God's original design, man was given power or dominion over all creation, but man forfeited that authority because of sin. Now, through Jesus Christ, the power that God designed for His followers has been restored. We possess authority over Satan and the forces of evil. But we struggle with this doctrinal truth because we don't feel like we have power. But Christ has given us the power to destroy strongholds in our lives and families and to preach the gospel to those living in darkness. Choosing to ignore the battle does not make the enemy go away. When we fight with our spouse or struggle with a rebellious child, we must realize that an enemy is attacking our family. We need to take authority in Jesus' name over the forces of darkness influencing our home.

Confession: Thank you, Father, for the power to tread on all the powers of the enemy.

July 9

Job 31-32; Acts 13:1-23

As they ministered

Acts 13:2
As they ministered to the Lord, and fasted, the Holy Ghost said, Separate me Barnabas and Saul for the work whereunto I have called them.

The Antioch church is a model for us today in the sense that they sought the Lord together. What is described here is a special term rarely seen in today's churches. We are busy doing a lot together. But rarely do we see the church ministering to the Lord and fasting. What does it mean to minister to the Lord? It simply means that they shared the word of God, prayed, worshipped, and listened to what God had to say as they fasted. God spoke to them through the Holy Spirit and revealed his plan and purpose as they did this. God is always willing to make his will known to us, but we are always busy doing so many things for God. Even in our prayer time, we should learn to be still and hear what the Holy Spirit says after our prayers.

Confession: Lord, I receive grace to be still and listen to what you have to say.

July 10

Job 33-34; Acts 13:24-52

Whenever you stand praying

Mark 11:25

And when ye stand praying, forgive, if ye have ought against any: that your Father also which is in heaven may forgive you your trespasses.

Our unforgiveness blocks our prayers from being answered. So now the question is, is this person, hurt, pain, and disappointment, worth my prayers not being answered? Only you can answer that question. The outcome is solely in your hands. It's not about anyone else but you. The power is in your hands. Unforgiveness is a wall that separates us from God. The only person who can tear down that wall is you. Unless we forgive freely, it shows that we have no consciousness of the grace that we received from God. When you hold somebody down in a spot, it's apparent that you will remain at the place to keep the person there. Therefore let go so that you can be free to move forward.

Confession: I will forgive everyone so that I will also receive forgiveness and move forward

July 11

Job 35-37; Acts 14

Pay your vows

Psalm 50:14-15

Offer unto God thanksgiving; and pay thy vows unto the most High: And call upon me in the day of trouble: I will deliver thee, and thou shalt glorify me.

The first thing that is listed in the scripture is thanksgiving. It is listed as a sacrifice to God. Taking time to say thank you is something many people do not do. How many people give thanks to God just for being able to get up in the morning? We need to thank God and give Him thanks for what He is doing in our lives throughout the day. Thank God for the little things, such as the air you breathe and being able to move. The second thing listed is for us to fulfill our vows to God. It is common for a person in a scary situation to promise God to do something for Him if He gets them out of the situation. Most people later forget about that vow or dismiss it as rash words said in the excitement. But the scripture above says we should call and expect God's deliverance when we have done these two things.

Confession: Help me, Lord, pay all my vows and be a man of integrity.

July 12

Job 38-39; Acts 15:1-21

Observe to do

Joshua 1:7
Only be thou strong and very courageous, that thou mayest observe to do according to all the law, which Moses my servant commanded thee: turn not from it to the right hand or to the left, that thou mayest prosper whithersoever thou goest.

To "be strong" speaks of an inner attitude, and "be courageous" speaks of outward behaviour. Joshua was told to be "very" strong and courageous. But not based on his strength and resources. But he would be "strong and courageous" so long as he was careful and observant to do according to all the law which Moses the servant of God commanded him to follow. Great boldness, courage, and strength come from knowing that you are right in the middle of God's revealed will and are doing as He commanded. But when you are acting in disobedience to God's clear will or are hesitating to do as you know He says to do, you find that you soon become very "afraid and dismayed.

Confession: Lord, I receive grace to observe to do as you have commanded.

July 13

Job 40-42; Acts 15:22-41

If you can believe

Mark 9:23
Jesus said unto him, If thou canst believe, all things are possible to him that believeth.

It was not Christ's ability to heal that was in question, for He created all things, and by Him, all things hold together. The man's faith in CHRIST had to be strong enough to receive from God. Thank God he was able to cry out, "Lord, I believe, help my unbelief", and he was rewarded with a son who was healed and restored. Faith sets no limit on God's ability for the one who is ready and willing to trust Him in all things. Jesus is the same yesterday, today, and forever, and His ability to heal the brokenhearted, cast out demons, set the captive free, make the lame to walk, the deaf to hear, and the dumb to speak has never diminished over time. As Jeremiah reminds us, "nothing is too difficult for God."But is your faith strong enough to receive from God?

Confession: Lord, I believe that you can do all things. You are the same yesterday, today, and forever.

July 14

Psalm 1-3; Acts 16:1-15

The word of God is life

John 6:63
It is the spirit that quickeneth; the flesh profiteth nothing: the words that I speak unto you, they are spirit, and they are life.

When we believe in the Lord Jesus Christ, we open the door for the Spirit to do His work. The Holy Spirit gives us life. He draws us to Christ and exalts Him as the living Lord. Jesus declares, "t*he words that I speak to you are spirit and are life".* God communicates life to us through His words. The word of God can give life to every situation. It is a powerful weapon given to the body of Christ. The word of God is quick and powerful, it carries creative virtues, and it is also medicinal according to Proverbs 4:20-22.

"But the flesh profits nothing", this means that human flesh and human nature do not profit. They cannot do anything to bestow eternal life. It is only in Christ Jesus that we have abundant life. The word of God will supply life to your flesh as you prophesy the healing scriptures every day.

Confession: Thank you, Father. I receive grace to prophesy your word every day.

July 15

Psalm 4-6; Acts 16:16-40

I know my sheep

John 10:27
My sheep hear my voice, and I know them, and they follow me:

Jesus is our caring Shepherd, Who guards and guides us. He feeds us and tends us. He loves and protects us, and He intimately knows each of His own by name. But do you know his voice? Hearing and recognizing the voice of our caring Shepherd comes from listening to His voice attentively – hearing the Word of God repeatedly and trusting the truth of all that He says. We are the sheep of His pasture, and we must be receptive to His call; we must carefully listen to all He says and trust all He does, even when we don't understand. The more we spend time fellowshipping with Him and listening to his word, the more familiar his voice becomes to us. Just as we easily recognize the voice of our earthly father having spent much time together.

Confession: I am your sheep lord. I will hear your voice and follow you always.

July 16

Psalm 7-9; Acts 17:1-15

By all means

2 Thessalonians 3:16

Now the Lord of peace himself give you peace always by all means. The Lord be with you all.

Do you have the peace of Christ over your head, like a roof that protects and guards you against being troubled and afraid? Are you experiencing a Shalom wholeness and tranquillity that is a gift to those who are trusting in the Lord of peace? Or is your peace being disturbed by circumstances or by issues of life. Do you find yourself worrying and anxious about the future (Health, finances, security, etc.)? Do anger and bitterness rob you of your inner tranquillity? Is there a particular person that you can't forgive, and it eats you up inside? Jesus promises His followers in John 14:27 "Peace I leave with you; my peace I give you. I do not give to you as the world gives. Do not let your hearts be troubled, and do not be afraid. God has made his peace available to his children. But it's our responsibility to receive the peace of God and refuse to be troubled or be afraid. He cares for us all.

Confession: Thank you, father, for your peace in my life.

July 17

Psalm 10-12; Acts 17:16-34

Jesus is the way

John 14:6
Jesus saith unto him, I am the way, the truth, and the life: no man cometh unto the Father, but by me.

Jesus did not simply say He would show us the way, but that He IS The Way. He is the only way for fallen man to get to the Father. And the way Jesus had to travel to that pivotal point in the history of the world was the way of the cross of Calvary, where His shed blood and selfless sacrifice shattered the immovable barrier between sinful man and a holy God. Yes! Jesus IS the only Way. Jesus is the personification of truth. Everything that is not of Christ is a lie, a deception, a distortion of truth, a half-truth, or partial truth. Jesus Christ is THE Life, Who breathes His own resurrected life into a fallen man, by faith. Every man is born spiritually dead in trespasses and sins and cannot save himself or communicate with a holy God. But Christ is the Source of all spiritual life and in Him is eternal life for all who trust in His redemptive work.

Confession: Jesus is my Lord and Savior, the only way to the Father.

July 18

Psalm 13-16; Acts 18

I will restore

Jeremiah 30:17
For I will restore health unto thee, and I will heal thee of thy wounds, saith the Lord; because they called thee an Outcast, saying, This is Zion, whom no man seeketh after.

This admonition is very important for us today because many hearts are wounded, depressed, and fearful due to the things happening in the world today. But God bids us here to raise our minds upwards to expect help from heaven, for there was none on earth that could heal the hearts of men. And he adds because they called thee, Zion, an outcast whom no one seeketh; that is, of whom, or whose welfare, no one cares about. The enemy wants God's people to be depressed and discouraged. But God promises that he will be our Redeemer. God promised to do the impossible, cure what is incurable, and heal what is beyond healing. To restore peace in our homes, To heal the wounded hearts. God is the great Physician of his people.

Confession: thank you, Father, for restoration.

July 19

Psalm 17-18; Acts 19:1-20

Great and mighty things

Jeremiah 33:3
Call unto me, and I will answer thee, and show thee great and mighty things, which thou knowest not.

God is willing to answer if we will humble ourselves and call upon him in prayer. When everything seems stacked against us, and all hope is lost, we begin to think that we are so utterly alone. We've tried everything we can think of, and still, we come up empty. It is precisely at times like these that we must prevail in prayer. We do not always see what God is doing behind the scenes. Yet, He invites us to call unto Him and trust Him anyway. He promises to show us great and mighty things. The great and mighty things are things you do not know or see. He is willing to bring healing, peace, restoration, and deliverance. We need to remember that He does the work of purging first before He brings about the work of deliverance. So wait and allow him to purge and cleanse you for the great and mighty things around that are to come.

Confession: Thank you, Father, for answering when I call.

July 20

Psalm 19-21; Acts 19:21-41

Death and life

Proverbs 18:21
Death and life are in the power of the tongue: and they that love it shall eat the fruit thereof.

We are reminded in this text that life and death are in the power of tongues, and whatever we speak will come to pass. Yes, we all will live with the consequences of our words, be it good or evil. What you say is what you get! This is why we MUST speak the Word of God out of our mouth concerning our families and in every circumstance we find ourselves. If you are a negative person and always talk about death, doubt, doom, and defeat in your life, that is what you will have. You hear some people say, "I can't do anything right". The proper confession should be, "I can do all things through Christ who strengthens me" (Philippians 4:13). Renew your mind through the Word of God daily and begin to say what God says concerning you. Remember, life and death are in the power of the tongue, and you will eat the fruit of your spoken words. Your life is what you speak it to be.

Confession: Lord, I receive grace to speak only positive words.

July 21

Psalm 22-24; Acts 20:1-16

Grieve not

Ephesians 4:30-31
And grieve not the holy Spirit of God, whereby ye are sealed unto the day of redemption. Let all bitterness, and wrath, and anger, and clamour, and evil speaking, be put away from you, with all malice:

What an assurance to know that God has sealed us with the Holy Spirit and will keep us sealed until Christ comes to claim us as His own. A seal is an official stamp on an important document - and the Spirit of God has officially sealed us. We are admonished not to grieve the Holy Spirit. This word reveals that God loves us. As Christians, the Holy Spirit is in us to help us, strengthen us, and teach and guide us. Therefore we must avoid the activities that grieve the Holy Spirit. Such as bitterness, anger, malice, and all fleshly activities. We hinder the flow and move of the Holy Spirit when we grieve him.

Confession: Help me, Lord, not grieve the Holy Spirit, my helper.

July 22

Psalm 25-27; Acts 20:17-38

His divine power

2 Peter 1:3
According as his divine power hath given unto us all things that pertain unto life and godliness, through the knowledge of him that hath called us to glory and virtue.

God's divine power has "granted to us all things that pertain to life and godliness," meaning that God has provided us with all we need for godliness. How do we obtain this gifted godliness? Peter tells us that it is "through the knowledge of him." We need to step into this glorious provision of abundant life, peace of mind, financial stability through the knowledge of God. The more you grow in the knowledge of God through the study and meditation of his word, the more like Jesus you become. Your understanding will also be enlightened, and you will be able to assess your divine inheritance in Christ. The Holy Spirit will give you ideas. He will open your eyes to see the Well by your side. A clearer knowledge of God brings greater joy in God.

Confession: Thank you, father, for your divine power that has given us all things that pertain to life.

July 23

Psalm 28-30; Acts 21:1-14

The blind leader

Matthew 15:14
Let them alone: they be blind leaders of the blind. And if the blind lead the blind, both shall fall into the ditch.

“And if the blind lead the blind, both shall fall into the ditch”. It was typical of the Jewish religious leaders to think of themselves as 'guides to the spiritually blind. But the fact is that, in reality, these religious leaders were themselves spiritually blind. Jesus Christ, the Son of God, was standing before them, yet they opposed Him in every way. They were so blind that they did not recognize the time of their visitation. We need to sharpen our spiritual perception as children of God by developing a deeper relationship with the Holy Spirit. You need spiritual discernment to recognize the spirit of deception that is in the world today because not all that profess to be Christian are true Christian. And If you are spiritually blind as a father, mother, pastor, or in any leadership position, you will lead your members into the ditch.

Confession: Lord, help me to develop a deeper relationship with you.

July 24

Psalm 31-33; Acts 21:15-40

Speak to your soul

Psalm 42:11
Why art thou cast down, O my soul? and why art thou disquieted within me? hope thou in God: for I shall yet praise him, who is the health of my countenance, and my God.

The Psalmist is discouraged by the things happening in his life. Biblically speaking, and ultimately there is no reason for a Christian to ever be without peace, comfort, joy, and happiness. This is because we have God, and He can't be taken away from us. The joy of the Lord is our strength. Though many of us may be going through difficult times right now, we have to move our perspective away from ourselves and focus on God and his kingdom. Then God will begin to do something great in our lives. One of the ways we change our focus and perspective is to meditate and listen to God's Word constantly. Many people depend on the things around them for happiness, but what happens when you are confronted with issues of life. That is why we need to allow the joy of the Lord to flow through us constantly.

Confession: Thank you for Father, the joy of the Lord is my strength.

July 25

Psalm 34-35; Acts 22

The apple of his eyes

Zachariah 2:8
For thus saith the Lord of hosts; After the glory hath he sent me unto the nations which spoiled you: for he that toucheth you toucheth the apple of his eye.

"For he that touches you touches the apple of his eyes". God calls His children the apple of His eye, or in another translation, the pupil of His eye, both of which mean something beautiful to God and carefully protected by Him. Harming God's chosen people is similar to striking the pupil of His eye. To mess with God's people is to mess with God. The word of God says in 2 Corinthians 11:2 That God is jealous over us with godly jealousy. Our God is jealous. He has redeemed us and brought us to Himself. He betrothed us to Himself through regeneration, and He wants us to be His chaste bride. The jealousy of God is like the jealousy of a husband over his wife; he would not let his wife be touched, go after another one, or have her heart occupied by anything other than him.

Confession: I am the apple of God's eye. I am untouchable.

July 26

Psalm 36-37; Acts 23:1-11

The sword of the spirit

Ephesians 6:17

And take the helmet of salvation, and the sword of the Spirit, which is the word of God

The weapon that we are to use to defeat all our foes in this earthly walk is the word of God, provided for us by our heavenly Father. The Holy Scriptures are divinely inspired by the Holy Spirit for doctrine, instruction, and correction. The word of God is the blade that will cut through every attack from the enemy. The word of God is living, powerful, and sharper than any two-edged sword, and every portion of the Scripture points to the Lord Jesus Christ, for He is the living Word. It was the sword of the Spirit that the Lord Jesus grasped when Satan tempted Him in the wilderness. Each time the enemy's subtle taunts, which were designed to cause Him to stumble in His mission, Jesus replied with the proclamation, "it is written". The word of God is the weapon of victory that we must grasp in our hands and our hearts, for with it, we can face every accusation of Satan and every doubt that is planted in our minds.

Confession: Thank you, Father, for your word. It is my weapon of victory.

July 27

Psalm 38-40; Acts 23:12-35

The angel's target

Psalm 34:7
The angel of the Lord encampeth round about them that fear him, and delivereth them.

This is an unfailing promise. God never leaves you to fend for yourself. He assures his protection to those who fear him. Fearing God doesn't mean being afraid of Him. Instead, it's demonstrating reverence or esteem and regard, love, and respect. The fear of the Lord is the beginning of wisdom. And as you do so, God's protection, favour, mercy, and kindness are released to you. But today, there's much more than angels guarding us as saints of God. The Bible describes Jesus as far superior to the angels (Hebrew 1:4). Jesus also said in Matthew 28:20, *"lo, I am with you always, even to* the *end of the age".* And when He left this earth after 33 years, he said, *""I will not leave you orphans…the Holy Spirit, whom the Father will send in My name, will always be with you".* He is right beside you. And if God is for you, who can be against you?

Confession: Thank you, father, I will beconscious of your divine presence.

July 28

Psalm 41-43; Acts

Power to witness

Acts 1:8
But ye shall receive power, after that the Holy Ghost is come upon you: and ye shall be witnesses unto me both in Jerusalem, and in all Judaea, and in Samaria, and unto the uttermost part of the earth.

The call to go into all the world as Christ's witnesses continue to be the Church's mission today. All Christians should consider themselves *sent* to witness what we have seen and heard about Jesus Christ. But Jesus told them they needed to wait until he sent his Holy Spirit. It was essential to understand that Jesus was not sending them alone or by their authority to preach, but that he would still be present in the ministry by His Spirit. By this, they would have the power to do what he did and say what he said. The Holy Spirit came on the day of Pentecost, and none of them was ever the same, having been empowered for life and ministry with the evidence of speaking in tongues. Are you empowered?

Confession: Lord, I receive the power to be your witness in Words and action.

July 29

Psalm 44-46; Acts 25

Due season

Galatians 6:9
And let us not be weary in well doing: for in due season we shall reap, if we faint not.

Paul encourages us as Christians not to be weary in well-doing. As Christians, we are called to "do good." This defines a broad range of services in the church and the world. Anything that builds and furthers the mission, expands the Kingdom and blesses the church and the world is "doing good."Jesus was going about doing good, and he expects us to do the same. We can get weary if we forget why we are doing it, or our motives become false. When you are doing good, you are obeying God, and in due season you will reap "If you faint not. Sometimes we feel that we are not appreciated for doing good. God will reward us here on earth at the proper time. And also, at the very latest, we will hear from the Lord, "Well done good and faithful servant" (Mt 25:21). We should look forward to this at the end of our days.

Confession: I will not be weary in well-doing. God will reward me in due season.

July 30

Psalm 47-49; Acts 26

Because He loves you

Deuteronomy 23:5
Nevertheless the Lord thy God would not hearken unto Balaam; but the Lord thy God turned the curse into a blessing unto thee, because the Lord thy God loved thee.

"Because the Lord thy God loved thee". Many of us do not realize how much God loves us. Even when the enemy fires his evil arrow, it will not come near you. But he can if you willingly open the door for him through unrighteous acts. The good word for today is that God blesses us and turns every cause into a blessing. This knowledge should enable us to make the best of every situation. It may seem strange and paradoxical, but in a way, a problem is the most creative force in this world. The pain of sickness built our hospitals. The blight of ignorance built our schools. Because walking was painful, we created ways to ride. Because cold winters were unpleasant, we created heat sources. Nearly every benefit we have has come as an effective response to some problem. God knows that our present problems can be future blessings.

Confession: Thank you, Lord, for turning every curse into a blessing.

July 31

Psalm 50-52; Acts 27:1-25

Search it out

Proverb 25:2

It is the glory of God to conceal a thing: but the honour of kings is to search out a matter.

God in His grace has shown us many things through nature, our inner conscience, and His God-breathed Word, but there are many secret things hidden from us within the created universe. Many glorious truths are hidden in the inerrant Word of God. But God has given us the Holy Spirit and the capacity to investigate, learn, and search out the truth - so that we can make sound judgments and provide wise counsel. The Holy Spirit searches out all deep things of God and shows us the things hidden within the word of truth. It is our honour to search out the hidden things. There are mysteries of the kingdom delivered to those who are willing to spend time with God, searching, meditating, and asking questions. You will find him if you seek him with all your heart.

Confession: I receive grace to keep on searching for the deep things of God.

August 1

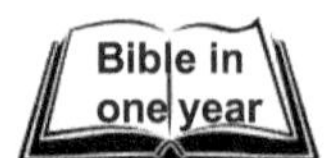

Psalm 53-55; Acts 27:26-44

By day and night

Exodus 13:21
And the Lord went before them by day in a pillar of a cloud, to lead them the way; and by night in a pillar of fire, to give them light; to go by day and night:

God has shown us very clearly in his word that he does not try to hide his will from us. He wants to lead us, guide us, and direct us every step, just like he did here. Now, you might think, well, I wish I had a pillar of cloud or a pillar of fire to lead me. But we have something so much better. We have the Holy Spirit of God living inside of us. God wants us to experience his will so much that he has come to live inside us to transform and direct our thoughts, desires, dreams, plans, and decision-making. What a glorious reality. We have the Spirit of God living inside of us. We've got something better than a pillar of cloud by day and a pillar of fire by night. God himself is permanently dwelling in all his children.

Confession: Thank you, father, for your divine presence.

August 2

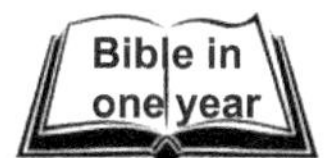

Psalm 56-58; Acts 28:1-15

The fruit of the Spirit

Galatians 5:22-23
But the fruit of the Spirit is love, joy, peace, longsuffering, gentleness, goodness, faith, meekness, temperance: against such there is no law.

The Fruit of the Spirit is a term that the apostle Paul uses to sum up nine visible attributes of the true Christian life. They are love, joy, peace, patience, kindness, goodness, faithfulness, gentleness, and self-control. These are physical manifestations of a Christian's transformed life. It is Christ living in us and transforming us. We can display this fruit only when we have Christ living in us. To have Christ living in us, we need to have a close relationship with Him. This is possible only if we spend time with Him through prayer, reading his word, and reflecting on it. Do you want to display more of the Fruit of the Spirit in your life? Then you can take nine days to reflect on each attribute of the Fruit of the Spirit. Note down your reflections and end with a prayer asking God to transform you to display that attribute in your life.

Confession: Help me, Lord, to display the nine fruits of the spirit.

August 3

Psalm 59-61; Acts 28:16-31

I live by faith

Galatians 2:20
I am crucified with Christ: nevertheless I live; yet not I, but Christ liveth in me: and the life which I now live in the flesh I live by the faith of the Son of God, who loved me, and gave himself for me.

All the law's demands were satisfied in Christ, who died under the law's penalty. They have no more hold on us because we are crucified with Him. Being crucified with Christ means that we are new creations. The dominating control of the fallen nature has been broken. If we do not understand this, we are missing something vital. The extinguished life means death to self and sin. The phrase "faith in the Son of God" mentioned above is loaded with rich meaning. We are to live by faith daily. Our desire should be for the one who gave himself for us. We must live for Christ by obeying the voice of the Holy Spirit. Paul says in the scripture above that the life he lives now is the life of faith in the Son of God.

Confession: Lord, help me to live for you every day.

August 4

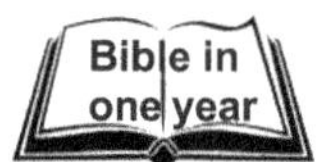

Psalm 62-64; Romans 1

The wisdom of God

1 Corinthians 1:21
For after that in the wisdom of God the world by wisdom knew not God, it pleased God by the foolishness of preaching to save them that believe.

For Christian men and women, the message of the Cross is the most glorious message of salvation - for the message of the cross is foolishness to those that are wise in their understanding, but to you and me, it is justification; sanctification; glorification and eternal union with Christ Jesus our Lord. God in His infinite wisdom has taken the prideful proclamations of fallen man and rendered them fools in His own eyes - for the fool has said in his heart there is no God, and in his pride, the wicked man does not seek after the Lord. For in all his thoughts, there is no room for the one true God, Creator of all. God sustains all things by the might of His magnificent power. But God in His infinite grace was pleased to save all who believe in the Cross of Christ.

Confession: Thank you, father, for, by Your grace and wisdom, You have given us Your gift of Salvation.

August 5

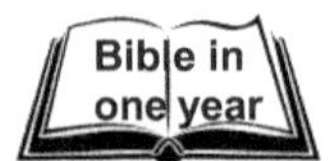

Psalm 65-67; Romans 2

I press on

Philippians 3:14
I press toward the mark for the prize of the high calling of God in Christ Jesus.

Each believer is called to run the race God has set before him. Every Christian has a specific purpose that God Himself has called them to achieve. We all have our own unique goal to attain, and that goal is purposed and planned by the Father, for it is God who works in each of His children both to will and to do that which pleases God. We need to align our goals with God's purpose for our lives. We can only do this as we spend time with him in the word and prayer. As we walk closely with God, he will lead us to where we should go. Apostle Paul said in the scripture above, "I press towards the mark." Paul had many things going on in his life, yet he could focus all his energies in one direction. He got rid of the distractions and concentrated on God's purpose for his life. Are you pressing towards the mark for the prize of your call?

Confession: I will not be distracted from the purpose of God for my life in Jesus' name.

August 6

Psalm 68-69; Romans 3

When you serve God

Exodus 23:25
And ye shall serve the Lord your God, and he shall bless thy bread, and thy water; and I will take sickness away from the midst of thee.

God warned the Hebrew people that they would be travelling through lands filled with foreign and false gods. He knew that they might be tempted to follow their ways and lifestyle, so he made them a promise with a blessing. Don't get distracted; worship and follow me, and I will bless your food, water, health, and productivity. This promise is for us today as Christians. God's blessing is upon us as long as we faithfully serve him. That is why we always give thanks over our meals because it is blessed. This scripture is also a weapon against sickness and deceases, for God promises to take sickness away from all his children. We need to be faithful in our service to God to enjoy all these blessings.

Confession: Help me, Lord, to serve you faithfully.

August 7

Psalm 70-72; Romans 4

Complete and equipped

2 Timothy 3:16-17
All scripture is given by inspiration of God, and is profitable for doctrine, for reproof, for correction, for instruction in righteousness: That the man of God may be perfect, thoroughly furnished unto all good works.

All 66 books of the Bible are God's unique resources to provide instruction and empower us to live out God's goodwill in our lives. There are many sources of knowledge around us. It increases day by day. But if you have a Bible, no matter how old and worn it may be, it outshines all the other resources one might have. To live extraordinary lives on earth, we need God's Word to give us a much greater understanding of His person, plans, and purposes. By instructing us of what exists and the purposes for which they exist. The word of God will teach us, correct us and prepare us for every good work. The one-year bible reading plan above will help you study at least three or four chapters daily. But you need discipline and determination to achieve it.

Confession: Lord, I ask that you will give me understanding as I study your word daily.

August 8

Psalm 73-74; Romans 5

He acknowledged God

Genesis 40:8
And they said unto him, We have dreamed a dream, and there is no interpreter of it. And Joseph said unto them, Do not interpretations belong to God? tell me them, I pray you.

I love the response of Joseph in this scripture. "Do not interpretations belong to God?" Then he said, "Please tell them to me." Joseph points the cup-bearer and the baker to God, who interprets dreams. He acknowledged that it was God who gave him the gift. Joseph had an unwavering faith in God even in a difficult situation. He must have been tempted to be mad at God because of the trials he was going through. When he fled from Potiphar's wife to avoid temptation, it got him into prison. His brothers also sold him into slavery because they were jealous of him. All this must have been a journey for Joseph. Yet, he left his pain and went about doing God's work. Let's drop our worries and pain at his feet and be a blessing to people. God knows how to fix it.

Confession: I will use my gift to serve you, Lord.

August 9

Psalm 75-77; Romans 6

Above all these things

Colossians 3:14
And above all these things put on charity, which is the bond of perfectness.

Love is the quality that binds all godly characteristics together in Christ. Love is the preeminent fruit of the Spirit from which all other virtues flow. Love bears all things, believes all things, hopes all things, endures all things - love never fails in God's economy. Other virtues may manifest, and different gifts may have been bestowed on a believer, but the Christian character is deeply flawed if godly love is lacking. True love is firmly secured to a committed affection and respect for the person. It is characterized by a wholehearted desire for the well-being of others. Love places God at the centre and circumference of our lives and gives Him the honour and respect due to His holy name. And the inflow of God's love into the life of a believer is transferred into an outflow of that love to others. Until you accept God's love, you cannot give love to others.

Confession: Lord, I accept your love. Help me to walk in love with others.

August 10

Psalm 78; Romans 7

Obedience and service

Job 36:11
If they obey and serve him, they shall spend their days in prosperity, and their years in pleasures.

Obedience is defined as doing what one is told to do. Obedience is our gateway to enjoying God's best. Our readiness and willingness to follow God's instruction put us in the position to be all that we are destined to be. God made us in His image and after His likeness. He gave us dominion over all He created. However, He left us with the choice to either follow His instruction or do as we please. Therefore, obedience is the tool that proves our choice to follow God or the devil in our daily lives. It is a ladder you have to climb in the development of character. To measure the strength of a person's character, check out their level of obedience to God's word in their daily affairs. It is your choices that show God your true intention and the attitude of your heart.

Confession: I will spend my days in prosperity because I obey and serve the Lord.

.

August 11

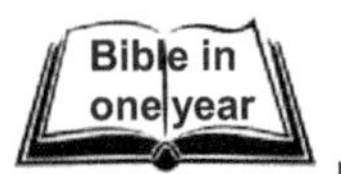

Psalm 79-81; Romans 8:1-18

God is our lifter

Psalm 3:3

But thou, O L*ORD, art a shield for me; my glory, and the lifter up of mine head.*

David wrote this psalm when he was driven from his throne, subjected to indescribable humiliation, by his son. Absalom's treachery and rebellion must have crushed David's heart. While David was fleeing from the armies of Absalom, broken by the spiteful betrayal of his child, he sat down and wrote the words of Psalm 3. David's anguish was undoubtedly magnified because his adversaries were primarily from his people. One of the primary tactics of such enemies is to undermine our faith in God to help us. David may well have been taunted with statements like: "where is your God now when you need him most?" Yet, in such affliction, accusation, and betrayal. David's cry is to the Lord, the covenant-keeping God. David knew that the hypnotic and paralyzing power of the enemy is broken only by turning one's gaze back to God, our lifter.

Confession: Thank you, Father, you are my glory and the lifter up of my head.

August 12

Psalm 82-84; Romans 8:19-39

It is by faith

Galatians 3:14
That the blessing of Abraham might come on the Gentiles through Jesus Christ; that we might receive the promise of the Spirit through faith.

Faith is used for the first time in Scripture in connection with Abraham. What made him so pleasing to God was that he believed in God and became the father of all those who believed.
Faith is that receptivity of the soul in which, as we draw near to God, His living power speaks to us. We yield ourselves, accepting His word and work in our lives. It has been said that faith is taking God at His word. We may have God's Word with all its promises at our disposal and yet fail to receive the blessing we seek. The faith that enters into the inheritance is the attitude of the soul that waits for God himself, first to speak His word and then to do what He has said. Faith is fellowship with God; it is surrender to God. Such was the faith that enabled Abraham to inherit the promises.

Confession: I will walk in faith and receive all my blessings.

August 13

Psalm 85-87; Romans 9

Clean yourself daily

John 15:3
Now ye are clean through the word which I have spoken unto you.

We are saved when we believe and confess Jesus Christ as our Lord and saviour. But for the rest of our lives, we are being sanctified as we are changed into His image and likeness. Jesus Christ explained that this is achieved aswe abide in Him and meditate on his word.
Day by day. We are to grow in grace and be changed from one state of glory to the next state of glory by the power of the indwelling Holy Spirit. At salvation, we are washed by the water of the Word of God and declared righteous by faith. However, throughout our earthly life, we are to continue to be cleaned day by day by the purifying effect of the Word of God in our life. We are to be daily cleansed by the washing of the water of the Word of God so that we may mature in the faith, grow in grace, and stand firm on the truth of the gospel of Christ.

Confession: I am cleansed daily as I meditate on the word of God.

August 14

Psalm 88-89; Romans 10

You need patience

Hebrews 10:36
For ye have need of patience, that, after ye have done the will of God, ye might receive the promise.

God's will refers to His moral commandments and priorities revealed in His Word. Under the pressure of trials, it is easy to justify moral compromise. Jesus resisted all compromise and steadfastly obeyed God's will, even when it meant a horrible death. We should also endure obeying God, even if it means suffering or going through persecution. After you have suffered, you will receive God's promise of salvation. But you need patience to receive God's promised salvation. You might have done the will of God, and yet there is no physical manifestation of your desires. The scripture above says that you need patience after doing the word of God. We are to Focus on always doing God's will, especially when trials tempt us to compromise. Let's live with an enduring faith in God, and He will sustain us through every trial.

Confession: I receive grace to be patient. God is faithful to fulfil His promises.

August 15

Psalm 90-92; Romans 11:1-21

You can save a soul

James 5:19-20
Brethren, if any of you do err from the truth, and one convert him; Let him know, that he which converteth the sinner from the error of his way shall save a soul from death, and shall hide a multitude of sins.

James is encouraging us here as believers to be our brother's keeper. If someone you know is straying from the truth, we are to reach out to them to help turn them back to the Lord. If you feel inadequate to do this, you should inform an elder who can guide you. But to ignore someone who is straying is like a member of the search and rescue team sitting at home watching TV while someone is lost in the woods. Rescue is required because they may be ashamed of what they've done, so they need to be assured of God's forgiveness if they will repent and confess their sins.

Confession: I will be my brother's keeper, I will point sinners to Christ

August 16

Psalm 93-95; Romans 11:22-36

Understanding is key

Matthew 13:23
But he that received seed into the good ground is he that heareth the word, and understandeth it; which also beareth fruit, and bringeth forth, some an hundredfold, some sixty, some thirty.

The hearer compared to good ground into which the seed fell is he that hears the word and understands it. Knowing the scripture is different from understanding it. Our spiritual understanding differentiates us from one another. Understanding brings enlightenment and quickening. The Holy Spirit will open your heart to receive the word of God with all readiness and meekness. You will be able to keep the word, hold it fast against all opposition, and bring forth fruit. Such a heareris the actual fruit of grace and righteousness from our Lord Jesus Christ, under the influences of the Spirit, through the word of God. We need to ask the Holy Spirit for understanding when reading the scripture.

Confession: Lord, I ask that you enlighten my eyes of understanding.

August 17

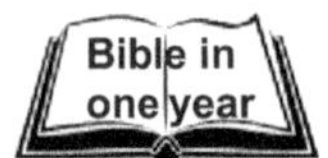

Psalm 96-98; Romans 12

The fear of people

1 Kings 12:26-27
And Jeroboam said in his heart, Now shall the kingdom return to the house of David: If this people go up to do sacrifice in the house of the Lord at Jerusalem, then shall the heart of this people turn again unto their lord, even unto Rehoboam king of Judah, and they shall kill me, and go again to Rehoboam king of Judah.

Jeroboam did not trust the Lord. God made him king, but he didn't trust God to keep him on the preserve him. We do this when we don't believe that God can save and preserve what he has given us. Jeroboam lost what he could have enjoyed from God. He was so privileged, and so are we. But he became afraid of the future took a wrong step, and made the people of God worship idols. Jeroboam led thepeople of God into idolatry, which is one of the greatest crimes possible. Rejecting Christ is the most foolish thing we can ever do when the door of mercy is wide open. We do not have to fear. We just have to trust God and believe that everything will work out for good if only we believe.

Confession: I will trust in the Lord always.

August 18

Psalm 99-102; Romans 13

Until Christ is formed

Galatians 4:19
My little children, of whom I travail in birth again until Christ be formed in you.

Paul had already gone through the 'birthing' experience with these believers when they were born again and brought into the family of God. But now, he is travailing in prayer. He is going through more excruciating birth-pains as he sought to bring them into spiritual maturity - until Christ is formed in them. Until he can see them being transformed into the image and likeness of the Lord Jesus Christ. Our transformation is in stages. Like newborn babies, we should desire the sincere milk of the word of God so that we can grow into maturity. We need to take our spiritual growth and our brothers and sisters in Christ seriously. We need to pray for one another so that Christ may be formed in us, to His praise and glory. May we die to self and live for Christ until by faith we are conformed into the image and likeness of Christ.

Confession: Help me, Lord, to travail in prayer for my brothers and sisters in Christ.

August 19

Psalm 103-104; Romans 14

One thing I do

Philippians 3:13
Brethren, I count not myself to have apprehended: but this one thing I do, forgetting those things which are behind, and reaching forth unto those things which are before.

Dwelling on past sins turns us in on ourselves rather than outward to Christ. Thinking over our past misdeeds, long since repented of, makes us self-centered; a constant turning overof silly acts or wrong decisions can make us downcast; swamp us with self-pity; produce a sense of frailty that cripples our spiritual outlook and hinders us from service; engulf us in shame and cause us to take our eyes off present and future spiritual realities. If God himself no longer remembers our sins and our iniquities (Jeremiah 31:34), it is ridiculous that we should drag them to the forefront of our thoughts. We need to take our eyes off the past and set them on the present reality of Christ, our representative. We need to lay hold on to the things that belong to us in Christ Jesus.

Confession: I will set my eyes on the present reality of Christ and the victory we have in him.

August 20

Psalm 105-106; Romans 15:1-21

Preparing for success

Joshua 1:8
This book of the law shall not depart out of thy mouth; but thou shalt meditate therein day and night, that thou mayest observe to do according to all that is written therein: for then thou shalt make thy way prosperous, and then thou shalt have good success.

The key to a prosperous life and good success is meditating on the book of the law, meditating on the word of God, and being careful to do according to what you read there. What does it mean to meditate? It means we don't just read the Bible. We soak it in. We let it become a part of us. We memorize it in some ways. We reflect on it in every way. The scripture above says that we will make our ways prosperous by observing to do what is written in the word. We need to recite His word in our hearts and keep the truth of His Word forever on our lips and in our hearts. For then, we will prosper and succeed in whatever we do to our benefit and His glory.

Confession: I receive grace to meditate on the word of God

August 21

Psalm 107-108; Romans 15:22-33

You can enter his rest

Hebrews 3:18-19
And to whom sware he that they should not enter into his rest, but to them that believed not? So we see that they could not enter in because of unbelief.

The entire nation of Israel fell into deliberate disobedience, apostasy, and unbelief, despite the fantastic miracles they had all witnessed in their lives. As children of God. The warning in this verse is not to fall into the same sin - not to be deliberately disobedient and wander into apostasy and unbelief. Blatant disobedience of God's word translates into 'unbelief.' For without faith, neither the lost sinner nor the saved saint can please God. How sad that the redeemed people of Israel were saved, but disobedience and unbelief left them living defeated lives. Instead of enjoying God's promised rest, they died defeated men and women - saved, yet excluded from His rest - redeemed from the slave market of sin, yet failing to fulfill God's will for their lives. You enter into his rest by believing God's word.

Confession: Lord, I believe in your word and in all you said concerning me.

August 22

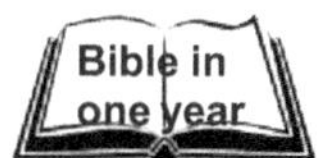

Psalm 109-111; Romans 16

Faith and action

James 2:20-21
But wilt thou know, O vain man, that faith without works is dead? Was not Abraham our father justified by works, when he had offered Isaac, his son upon the altar?

Abraham's faith was "active along with his works." Abraham's prior exercise of saving faith had set him in right standing with God. But his faith was not invisible until it showed itself in the works that it inherently contained. James here describes faith as being "completed" by Abraham's action. Abraham's visible obedience emerged from his invisible saving faith and demonstrated said faith in the visual realm. As such, he was "justified," shown to be righteous by a living faith that led to obedience. As the body apart from the spirit is dead, so also faith apart from works is dead". Living faith is an active faith. If you truly believe in God, you will take action concerning those things the Holy Spirit laid in your heart.

Confession: I believe in God, I will take action inJesus' name.

August 23

Psalm 112-115; 1 Corinthians 1

We have boldness

Hebrews 10:19
Having therefore, brethren, boldness to enter into the holiest by the blood of Jesus.

As children of the most high God, we have confidence in approaching the presence of God. We have "boldness to enter into the holy place." This boldness is holy freedom of access to God because of our assurance that he shall graciously receive us. We may freely express our wants and wishes to our heavenly Father. What a great privilege we have to call on our heavenly Father any time of the day. Hewill not resent our confidence but will welcomeus more because of it. It is by the sacrifice of Christ that we have the right of access to the presence of God. And it is by the infinite love of God manifested in that sacrifice that wehave confidence in availing ourselves of this right. This great privilege has been obtained for us through the mediation of our Lord Jesus Christ.

Confession: Thank you, Father, for the boldness to come into your presence.

August 24

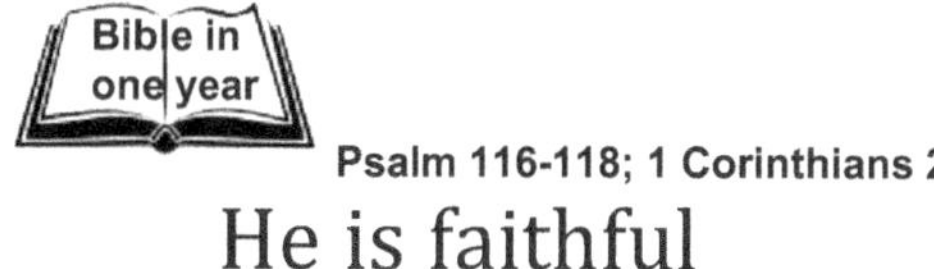

Psalm 116-118; 1 Corinthians 2

He is faithful

1Thessalonians 5:24
Faithful is he that calleth you, who also will do it.

Down through the generations, God has proved Himself faithful, and down through those same ages, God has been working towards His perfect plan and purpose for humanity, which is Christ in us the hope of glory. And the work that He wants to do in the lives of each of His children is to transform us into the image and likeness of our Lord Jesus Christ - spirit, soul, and body. And so we are called upon to live as unto the Lord in the power of the Holy Spirit - to be at peace knowing that faithful is he that has called us. We are to rejoice always, to pray constantly, and to give thanks in everything - knowing that this is God's will for each of His children. God, Himself will carry out all the work needed to bring us into spiritual maturity Himself - we need to rest in His love and yield to the work of His Spirit in the inner man.

Confession: Thank You, Father. You can perfect all that concerns me.

August 25

Psalm 119:1-48; 1 Corinthians 3

Mark the perfect man

Psalm 37:37
Mark the perfect man, and behold the upright: for the end of that man is peace.

The word "perfect" here is used to designate a righteous man or a man who serves and obeys God. The word "mark" here means "observe, take notice of." The argument is, "Look upon that man, in the end, take notice of him: he is perfect in his soul, God has saved him from all sin and filled him with his love and image." And he is upright in his conduct. His end is peace, quietness, and assurance forever. The psalmist points out here that there is an advantage in serving God faithfully. God is the friend of the righteous. Sometimes it seems like it doesn't pay to be good! When the evil prosper and the good suffers, you can be tempted to doubt God's faithfulness. The scripture above says that the end of the perfect man is peace. God is not unrighteous. He will grant you peace in every aspect of your life.

Confession: I receive grace to live a righteous life. I speak peace to every aspect of my life.

August 26

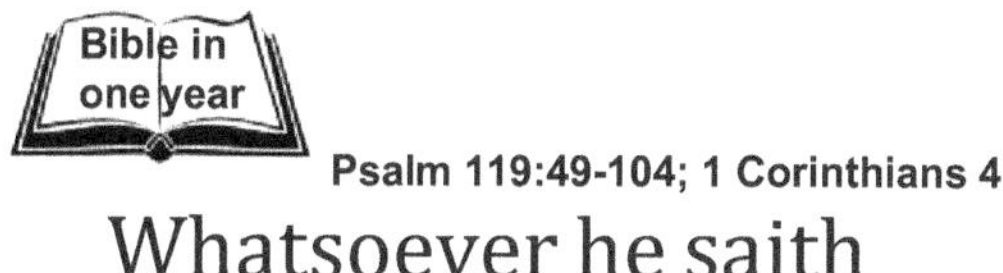

Psalm 119:49-104; 1 Corinthians 4

Whatsoever he saith

John 2:5
His mother saith unto the servants, Whatsoever he saith unto you, do it.

Mary must have pondered on the gracious words and godly wisdom she heard from Jesus daily. She understood what we all have to learn - that there is an unbridgeable gulf between God and man, which only the Lord Jesus can span. I believe her trust and confidence in Jesus made her approach him for a solution. Mary did what we are all called to do - she pointed others to God's only begotten Son. She directed their attention away from herself to the Lord Jesus Christ. "*Whatsoever he saith unto you, do it.*" The word "whatsoever" means that we must obey Him without questioning or dispute. Fancy being told to fill the waterpots with water when wine was needed! Fancy being told to bear water to the governor of the feast! Yet they gave the Lord their unquestioning obedience.

Confession: Lord, I will do what you ask me to do without questioning.

August 27

Psalm 119:105-176; 1 Corinthians 5

I will make darkness light

Isaiah 42:16

And I will bring the blind by a way that they knew not; I will lead them in paths that they have not known: I will make darkness light before them, and crooked things straight. These things will I do unto them, and not forsake them.

God is willing to take us by the hand and show us the way. He has promised not to forsake us. He delivered us from our enemies despite our repeated waywardness. God gave us his word to supply all we need for emotional and spiritual health. God is faithful to his children. He is willing to stick with us even in our unfaithfulness. He will not leave us for a moment, no matter how far off track we've gone. God wants us to know that he has already prepared a way of escape when we are hoping beyond hope. What difference would it make in our lives if we could trust in a God who loves us that much, who is waiting for us to take his proffered hand and walk with him.

Confession: I will trust in you Lord, I will not be afraid.

August 28

Psalm 120-121; 1 Corinthians 6:1-10

Fulfill your promise

Deuteronomy 23:23
That which is gone out of thy lips thou shalt keep and perform; even a freewill offering, according as thou hast vowed unto the Lord thy God, which thou hast promised with thy mouth.

A vow is a solemn promise or assertion by which a person is bound to act on one's commitment or perform or render a service or meet a condition attached to the promise. It is a personal prayer to God or an individual backed up by integrity to fulfil one's part in the bargain. It takes integrity, fear of God, and honesty to fulfil a vow. People vow for circumstantial reasons, especially when in trouble. We must fulfil our vows to God. There are consequences when you purposely refuse to pay your vow to God. Vows must not be negative to God's laws and commandments. We all should be strong in the Lord to break all negative vows we made in ignorance or before we came to Christ.

Confession: I will pay all my vows. I will keep my integrity.

August 29

Bible in one year

Psalm 121-123; 1 Corinthians 6:11-20

Things that defile a man

Matthew 15:18
But those things which proceed out of the mouth come forth from the heart; and they defile the man.

The Pharisees and scribes were all concerned about the outsides. They wanted everybody to keep the tradition. They were concerned with trying to clean up the outside. But Jesus was concerned with getting to the root of the problem. The source of defilement isn't from outside of us. The source of defilement comes from within; it comes from our heart. Jesus points out that it isn't what and how you eat that renders you clean or unclean. It is what and how you speak that renders you clean or unclean. How do you react under pressure? The book of James 3:8 taught us how deadly the tongue is. He said, "No one can tame the tongue. It is a restless evil and full of deadly poison." Our tongues can fire off poisonous darts that wound people incredibly.

Confession: Help me, Lord, to speak words that will bless people.

August 30

Psalm 124-127; 1 Corinthians 7:1-24

Fear has torment

Psalm 56:3-4
What time I am afraid, I will trust in thee. In God I will praise his word, in God I have put my trust; I will not fear what flesh can do unto me.

"What time I am afraid," verse three says, "I will trust in thee." So when you are afraid, lift your eyes to God and say, "I trust in you." B When we have our eyes fixed on the things that are happening around us in the world or something that men or women can do to us, then there's a reason for fear, but not when we lift our eyes to the Lord our God. How do you get from when I am afraid not to be afraid? Here's how you put your trustin God. You prophesy His word, and you trust that He is all that His word says He is. Why dowe prophesy His word? Because His word is filled with promises that can help us overcomefear. Promises like Romans, chapter eight. "If God is for us, who can be against us?" Fill your mind and your heart when you are tempted to be afraid with promises from God'sword.

Confession: Thank you, Father, you are all your word says you are.

August 31

Psalm 128-131; 1 Corinthians 7:25-40

Take heed

1 Corinthians 10:12
Wherefore let him that thinketh he standeth take heed lest he fall.

We are indeed privileged to be saved by grace through faith in Christ and to have been freed from the curse of the Law through His sacrificial death and glorious resurrection - but we must maintain an attitude of eschewing that which is evil and seeking to do that which is righteous in the eyes of the Lord.
1 Thessalonians 5:22 warns us to abstain from all appearances of evil. You can imagine a Christian brother living together with a Christian sister in the same apartment, and they are not legally married. Such should not be mentioned among us as believers.
However, there is nothing that can separate us from the love of God in Christ Jesus our Lord. But we must be aware that any one of us may be tempted to fall into sin - and should we become over-confident in our spiritual walk, the danger of falling into sin is significantly increased.

Confession: Help me, Lord, to abstain from all appearance of evil.

September 1

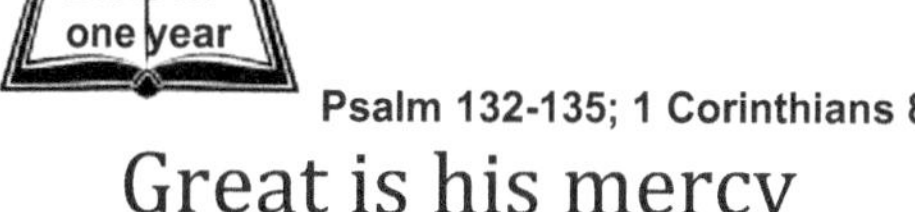

Psalm 132-135; 1 Corinthians 8

Great is his mercy

Psalm 103:11-12
For as the heaven is high above the earth, so great is his mercy toward them that fear him. As far as the east is from the west, so far hath he removed our transgressions from us.

The psalmist here talks about God's mercy. His mercy has brought us into a new month. God's mercy is "as high as the heaven is above the earth." Again, we have a statement of overwhelming magnitude, something that would have truly been incalculable and unimaginable to the ancients. No matter how far up a person could go, he would never outdistance God's mercy. When God forgives, He forgives completely. Our sins have been removed from us as far as possible to imagine. It is a statement of complete and utter forgiveness. Once our sins have been removed, we will never be held accountable for them. They will never come back to haunt us. (Romans 8:1) says, "Therefore, there is now no condemnation for those who are in Christ Jesus.

Confession: Thank you, Father, for your mercy towards us.

September 2

Psalm 136-138; 1 Corinthians 9

He drove them all out

John 2:15
And when he had made a scourge of small cords, he drove them all out of the temple, and the sheep, and the oxen; and poured out the changers' money, and overthrew the tables.

God purposed the House of the Lord to be a place of prayer for all nations, but the priests and rulers of the people had defiled this holy place and turned God's dwelling into a den of thieves and a hideout for bandits. Our Lord Jesus is seen here cleansing the Temple of God from the many ungodly practices implemented over the years. Like he cleansed the physical temple, he is also doing so today. When we open the door of our heart for him, he comes in and drives away all that is buying and selling because we are the temple of God. When there is an entrance of the wordof God, light comes with understanding which brings deliverance. So stay on the word until the light comes.

Confession: Thank you, Father. I will stay onthe word until the light comes.

September 3

Psalm 139-141; 1 Corinthians 10:1-13

He will hide you

Psalm 31:20
Thou shalt hide them in the secret of thy presence from the pride of man: thou shalt keep them secretly in a pavilion from the strife of tongues.

God has promised to hide us from our enemies and brings us into the very place where He dwells. He wants us to be before Him and near Him. His is always with us, and we can be confident of His protection. Many times when we talk of enemies, we think of human beings. But our primary enemy is the devil. He comes with sickness and diseases. He can even influence your loved ones against you. The bible says that we wrestle not against flesh and blood but against principalities and powers (Ephesian 6:12). When the wicked form a conspiracy or enter into a league against the righteous, God will take the righteous, as it were, into His immediate presence and will protect them.

Confession: Thank you, Father, for keeping me from the strife of tongues.

September 4

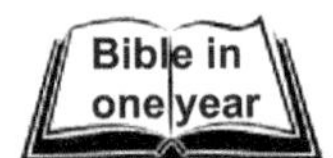

Psalm 142-144; 1 Corinthians 10:14-33

Treasure in earthen vessels

2 Corinthians 4:7
But we have this treasure in earthen vessels, that the excellency of the power may be of God, and not of us.

Only the gospel treasure reveals God's plan for man's redemption (Romans 1:15-17). The gospel of Christ is the unique "*power of God to salvation*" (Romans 1:16). The gospel is the sole message that can be obeyed, with the result being that those who obey are saved. Only the gospel is sealed by the blood of Christ (Matthew 26:28). It is a treasure, indeed! The gospel is preached through God's faithful servants, who are His earthen vessels. Like the early disciples, we must go everywhere preaching the gospel of Christ.. God depends on you and me to tell the lost about Jesus. You can preach Christ through your character. You can also preach Christ through your talent, like composing songs that point people to Christ. Let us use every opportunity to spread the gospel of Christ.

Confession: I will preach Christ with every opportunity I have with My character.

September 5

Psalm 145-147; 1 Corinthians 11:1-15

He will do a new thing

Isaiah 43:18-19

Remember ye not the former things, neither consider the things of old. Behold, I will do a new thing; now it shall spring forth; shall ye not know it? I will even make a way in the wilderness, and rivers in the desert.

This is a warning from the Lord "Remember ye, not the former things, neither consider the things of old. Behold, I will do a new thing. God loves doing new things. He is making a path through the wilderness. He is causing the stream to flow through the desert instead of dwelling in the past at everything wrong. Ask instead for your eyes to be open to what he is doing. just because we cannot see God's blessings at work does not mean he is not knitting our life together. " If we want to grow into a closer walk with Him, we're going to have to allow God to lead us in places we've never been before; God is already at work whether we see it or not. There is a wilderness, but God is building a path. There is a dessert, but a stream is flowing.

Confession: Lord, I believe your word. You are knitting my life together.

September 6

Psalm 148-150; 1 Corinthians 11:16-34

But my God

Philippians 4:19
But my God shall supply all your need according to his riches in glory by Christ Jesus.

When Paul says, "my God shall supply all your need," he is authoritatively putting before us the only true God, the God who has proven reliability. We should be glad to put our trust in *that* God. Sometimes, we need material provision. And God is abundantly able to provide that and will do so whenever needed. But He may not offer it through money. He may provide it through someone else meeting the need in some other way. Or He may provide a change of the circumstances; so that the need becomes no longer needed. Sometimes, what we need is courage; and God will provide that. Sometimes, patience is required, and God will provide that. Sometimes, we need peace, maturity, steadfastness, or the ability to love someone difficult. God will provide for all of these needs too.

Confession: Thank you, father, for supplying all my needs.

September 7

Proverbs 1-2; 1 Corinthians 12

When you observe

Deuteronomy 28:1
And it shall come to pass, if thou shalt hearken diligently unto the voice of the Lord thy God, to observe and to do all his commandments which I command thee this day, that the Lord thy God will set thee on high above all nations of the earth.

God blesses us with abundant blessings. Salvation positions us for blessing. When you are positioned through redemption, then your lifestyle of obedience to the voice of God allows God to bless you supernaturally beyond anything you could do for yourself. We are blessed when we obey God's commands. God always commands; he never begs. He commands all people everywhere to repent" (Acts 17:30). He also commands us to believe and to love one another: "And this is his command: to believe in the name of his Son, Jesus Christ, and to love one another as he commanded us." As many that will obey this command will be supernaturally blessed.

Confession: Lord, help me to open the door of blessing by obeying your commands.

September 8

Proverbs 3-4; 1 Corinthians 13

Think on these things

Philippians 4:8
Finally, brethren, whatsoever things are true, whatsoever things are honest, whatsoever things are just, whatsoever things are pure, whatsoever things are lovely, whatsoever things are of good report; if there be any virtue, and if there be any praise, think on these things.

Paul here gives us a way to combat Satan's efforts. We are to feed our minds with blessings from God and the good things we can find in our lives or situations. We are to think about what is true rather than the lies Satan would have us believe. We are to dwell on what is noble and right so our actions will follow our thoughts. We are to feed our minds with whatever is pure, lovely, admirable, excellent, or praiseworthy—all the things that help us stay focused on God's love for us and Christ's sacrifice for us. As we actively practice this, we can fight painful situations, trials, and all the difficult things we face, even in the most challenging moments.

Confession: I will think about things that are true, lovely, and of good report.

September 9

Proverbs 5-6; 1 Corinthians 14:1-20

The word of God will build you

Acts 20:32
And now, brethren, I commend you to God, and to the word of his grace, which is able to build you up, and to give you an inheritance among all them which are sanctified.

Here Paul commands us"to the word of his grace." There is a difference between "grace." and "the word of his grace." Nothing but grace can save the soul – nothing but super-abounding grace can blot out and hide our aggravated iniquities from the view of justice. But "the word of his grace" is that word that brings this grace into the heart, which communicates life and power to the soul. It is that which the Spirit, by his inward teaching and testimony, seals on the conscience. It is "the word of God's grace," communicated to the soul out of Christ's inexhaustible and divine fullness that alone builds up. All other building is baseless fabric, a mere 'house of cards. We must feed our spirit man daily with the word of God.

Confession: Help me, Lord, love your word more than my daily bread.

September 10

Proverbs 7-8; 1 Corinthians 14:21-40

You can prolong your days

Exodus 20:12
Honour thy father and thy mother: that thy days may be long upon the land which the Lord thy God giveth thee.

Honouring one's father and mother is obedient to them, listening to their advice, and complying with their instructions. The Lord has charged parents to train up a child in the way they should go and help shape appropriate behaviours and attitudes towards other people and their understanding of God and His plan of salvation. Though it is the responsibility of all parents and guardians to teach their children the fear and nurture of the Lord, all children also must take this vital instruction to heart, to honour and care for their parents even when we feel that our guardian or parents did not fulfil their God-given responsibility. Those who reverence God by obeying His command to honour their father and mother have the assurance that they will live long in the land the Lord their God has given them.

Confession: I will honour my parents and guardian. I will care for them until old age.

September 11

Proverbs 9-10; 1 Corinthians 15:1-32

God meant it for good

Genesis 50:20
But as for you, ye thought evil against me; but God meant it unto good, to bring to pass, as it is this day, to save much people alive.

Joseph is a beautiful picture of the Lord Jesus. He was loved by his father; hated by His brethren; betrayed by those He knew and loved – only to be used by God to save His people from death and destruction. He was later placed in the highest position in the land, Having passed all the trials he was confronted with. When evil and distressing situations happen to us or our personal plans, we have several choices we can wallow in the slough of despond and murmur against God for our misfortune and bemoan our sorry state as we become embittered with our lot or, by faith, we can rest in the promises of God, knowing that no matter what happens in this life, God will bring good out of evil. Just as in the life of Joseph, his brothers meant it for evil, but God turned it around for good. Relax. God is on your side.

Confession: Thank you, father, all things are turning around for my good.

September 12

Proverbs 11-12; 1 Corinthians 15:33-58

Walk in the spirit

Galatians 5:16-17

This I say then, Walk in the Spirit, and ye shall not fulfil the lust of the flesh. For the flesh lusteth against the Spirit, and the Spirit against the flesh: and these are contrary the one to the other: so that ye cannot do the things that ye would.

Walking in the Spirit is a conscious process that has to go on as we go about our daily activities. It means submitting ourselves to the influence of the Holy Spirit to guide us and to lead us. Such submission can begin each day with a simple, heartfelt prayer: "Lord, I realize that I cannot live a holy life without your help. And so I submit myself to the Holy Spirit's leading". When you make this prayer every day, you will find an unusual ability that you did not have before to produce the fruit of the Spirit mentioned in verses 22,23 of our passage. Besides these things, when you walk in the Spirit, you will also find that you have an enhanced desire to obey God and please Him, rather than please yourself in whatever you do.

Confession: Lord, help me to always walk in the spirit.

September 13

Proverbs 13-14; 1 Corinthians 16

Submit and resist

James 4:7
Submit yourselves therefore to God. Resist the devil, and he will flee from you.

James gives us various steps to achieving a spiritual walk. Including submission to God, drawing near to our heavenly Father, humbling ourselves before the mighty hand of God and not giving Satan a foothold in our life. But one very important exhortation is to resist the devil, and he will flee from us. To overcome the enemy's temptations, we are instructed to resist the devil, resist the temptation, resist the sin, and resist the evil. When temptation hammers on the door of our mind, we are simply to say NO! We are to decline that sinful temptation and turn down that lustful desire. But the strength to resist comes from submitting to God's will, God's way, God's instruction, and his word. You cannot resist the devil without submitting to God. Many Christians are not submitting to God's word and his ways. How then can we resist the devil?

Confession: I will submit myself to God in all things.

September 14

Proverbs 15-16; 2 Corinthians 1

He has prepared a table

Psalm 23:5
Thou preparest a table before me in the presence of mine enemies: thou anointest my head with oil; my cup runneth over.

Here, David's word for "table" refers specifically to a table spread with food. This is not a table used as a desk or for storage, but David talks about a meal. This is a banquet table, where you share fellowship with the host and his other guests. The Lord "prepares" this table for us even in the presence of our enemies. The word "prepare" means "to arrange," to set out or put in order. God has arranged a table for you even in your present condition. Don't focus on the issue; instead, focus on God. The enemies have to be there to witness what God is about to do in your life. The enemies have to be there to push Joseph into his divine destiny. Don't pray for your enemies to die. They are part of the process. One day the enemies of God will look on as God honours his people in their presence.

Confession: Thank you, Lord, I see a table prepared before me

September 15

Proverbs 17-18; 2 Corinthians 2

Don't forget

James 1:23-24
For if any be a hearer of the word, and not a doer, he is like unto a man beholding his natural face in a glass: For he beholdeth himself, and goeth his way, and straightway forgetteth what manner of man he was.

We all take time to look into the mirror every day. The mirror will reveal every dirty spot and smudge, every mole and wrinkle, every receding hairline or hair on our face that needs to be removed. The Word of God is like a mirror that shows us our spiritual self, our inner man, which we could not see otherwise. And the Word of God, which is a mirror to our soul, flatters no man. It reveals our sin and how we have missed the mark. James points out that anyone who is a hearer and not a doer of the word is like he who looks at the mirror and forgets how he looks. But the person who pays close attention, looks intently at the perfect law of liberty, does the work of obedience, and does not forget what he has heard, this man will be blessed in what he does.

Confession: I receive grace to be the hearer and doer of God's word.

September 16

Proverbs 19-20; 2 Corinthians 3

Focus on things that edify

1 Corinthians 10:23
All things are lawful for me, but all things are not expedient: all things are lawful for me, but all things edify not.

Paul's focus here is on how we exercise our Christian liberties. Paul tells us to consider whether our lawful actions are beneficial and constructive to help others. Though it may be legal to perform a particular act, the circumstances surrounding it may not help our brothers and sisters in Christ. Even if not a sin, we still must consider whether we are promoting the welfare of others before we act. Paul says that even though something is legal, you should consider the effect on others before doing it. Paul concludes in verse 31 of the above scripture whatever you do, do all to the glory of God. So, this would include partially matters of conscience, how should I educate my children, what music may I listen to, what television shows or movies may I watch, should I smoke tobacco or drink alcohol. Our criterion is, does this bring glory to God?

Confession: I will do all things to the glory of God.

September 17

Proverbs 21-22; 2 Corinthians 4

Maturity

Philippians 3:15-16
Let us therefore, as many as be perfect, be thus minded: and if in any thing ye be otherwise minded, God shall reveal even this unto you. Nevertheless, whereto we have already attained, let us walk by the same rule, let us mind the same thing.

Attitudes are the flavour–they make life fun, strengthening you when life gets rough. Attitudes are the spice that makes good times sweeter and bad times an adventure. Attitudes are the boost in God's grace, the cup of cold water amid the marathon race. But with the wrong attitudes, you will hit the wall and collapse. We need to cultivate the right attitudes, If we're going to grow, mature, become godly, and be impactful for Christ. The word "as many as are perfect" here means the mature, full-grown in contrast to babes, total, wholeness, grown-up, full age, full-grown man, mature man in Christ. This is someone who seeks to live by the Word of God in every aspect of their life.

Confession: Help me, Lord, to maintain a good attitude and grow in Christ.

September 18

Proverbs 23-24; 2 Corinthians 5

God is concerned

Exodus 2:25
And God looked upon the children of Israel, and God had respect unto them.

While the Israelite's certainly wondered whether or not God was hearing, He *did* hear their groaning. And He always hears our cries. The one who loves us, "He who has ears. Not only does God hear us when we cry out to him, but he also cares for us. But sometimes, when the challenges of life pressure us, we wonder if God hears our cry. The word of God says in (Isaiah 49: 14-16a) Can a woman forget her nursing child, that she should have no compassion on the son of her womb? Even these may forget, yet I will not forget you. Behold, I have engraved you on the palms of my hands. This is the word of God to all who are willing to stretch out their faith and hold unto the word of God. (NLT) translation of the passage above says He looked down on the people of Israel and knew it was time to act. I believe it is time for God to act in your favour.

Confession: Thank you, father, it's my time of visitation.

September 19

Proverbs 25-27; 2 Corinthians 6

Accepted religion

James 1:26-27

If any man among you seem to be religious, and bridleth not his tongue, but deceiveth his own heart, this man's religion is vain.
Pure religion and undefiled before God and the Father is this, To visit the fatherless and widows in their affliction, and to keep himself unspotted from the world.

James here talks about “pure and undefiled religion” from two standpoints—first in terms of what it isn’t, and then in terms of what it is, or as we might put it, the “don’t” and the “do” of true religion. James talks of someone who “thinks he is religious and does not bridle his tongue. ” To “bridle” the tongue is a figure of speech for bringing the tongue under control. The truth is that the product of the mouth betrays what’s really in the heart—such things as lying, filthy talk, speaking evil of other people. James also shows us the true expression of religion that God would accept as “pure and undefiled.” It must be characterized by an open hand to those in need. It must also be characterized by a holy life.

Confession: Lord, help me to be a blessing to people.

September 20

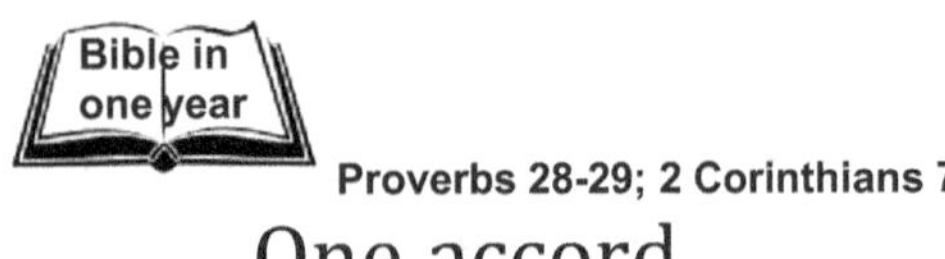

Proverbs 28-29; 2 Corinthians 7

One accord

Acts 2:46-47
And they, continuing daily with one accord in the temple, and breaking bread from house to house, did eat their meat with gladness and singleness of heart, Praising God, and having favour with all the people. And the Lord added to the church daily such as should be saved.

We see in the scripture above that these Jerusalem Christians were all of one mind, that they were experiencing a remarkable unity. 'Singleness of heart", Their hearts, as it were, were melted into one another. Our Lord had prayed that his disciples might be one, even as he and his Father were one (John:17:21), and here they were giving expression to this oneness. They had different temperaments, different backgrounds, different upbringings. They differed in almost every conceivable way, yet they were all melted into one in this extraordinary unity. It is an excellent principle that when men and women believe the Christian gospel, the main effect it has upon them is to unify their life, to make them 'single.' Christ should be the centre of all we do.

Confession: Lord, help your church to be one indeed.

September 21

Proverbs 30-31; 2 Corinthians 8

We are silted in heavenly places

Ephesian 2:6

And hath raised us up together, and made us sit together in heavenly places in Christ Jesus:

We have a new and eternal position simply because we believe in Jesus. We have been positioned in Christ and exalted together with Him into heavenly places in him. While positionally and spiritually, we are already seated together with Christ in the heavenly realms, our physical condition may seem to contradict the truth of our new position in Him. We died with Christ and are dead to the world, and our life is hidden in Him, yet we are to put to death the things of the world and the lust of the flesh. There is no contradiction in God's Word. Since God raised us with Christ and seated us with Him in the heavenly realms, we ought to live our lives by faith, with thanksgiving, in a manner worthy of our exalted position in Christ and glorifies our Father Who is in heaven.

Confession: Thank you, father, that we are seated with Christ in heavenly places

September 22

Ecclesiastes 1-3; 2 Corinthians 9

God is preparing you

Genesis 39:20
And Joseph's master took him, and put him into the prison, a place where the king's prisoners were bound: and he was there in the prison.

Trials come more home to us when someone for whom we care, or perhaps ourselves, "endure grief, suffering wrongfully." We feel not only that wrong has been done, but as if there had been a failure in God's care. Sometimes we think of suffering as calling for immediate restitution for our wrong actions. But sometimes, God is carrying out a plan, we may not be able to trace it, but it is so. Thus it was with Joseph. Though he was punished unjustly, Joseph continued to be strengthened in his interest and concern for other people when he could have been sulking and exclusively concerned about himself. Every challenging experience enriched Joseph's character and prepared him for his divine assignment. God is behind the scene, working for your good.

Confession: Help me, Lord, to stand firm in faith no matter the situation.

September 23

Ecclesiastes 4-6; 2 Corinthians 10

You are sealed

2 Corinthians 1:22
Who hath also sealed us, and given the earnest of the Spirit in our hearts.

At the moment of salvation, we were sealed. God's seal on His children is a stamp of ownership. We are no longer part of the satanic kingdom of darkness but a member of Christ's body, having been transferred into the kingdom of His dear Son - and having become children of the light, by faith. The seal of God on each believer confirms our union with Christ and our identity as God's purchased possession, for we were bought with a price - the precious blood of Jesus Christ our God and Saviour. God gave the Spirit of promise into our hearts as a down payment or as an insurance policy - to underscore the indestructible substance of His Word. The eye has not seen, and the ear has not heard the wonders that God has prepared for His purchased possession - who have not only been sealed by Him but also have the indwelling Holy Spirit of promise in their heart.

Confession: Thank you, father, you have securely sealed me as Your promised possession.

September 24

Ecclesiastes 7-9; 2 Corinthians 11:1-15

God is our deliverer

Exodus 3:8

And I am come down to deliver them out of the hand of the Egyptians, and to bring them up out of that land unto a good land and a large, unto a land flowing with milk and honey; unto the place of the Canaanites, and the Hittites, and the Amorites, and the Perizzites, and the Hivites, and the Jebusites.

Our heavenly father sees the affliction of His children. He hears the cry of His people, and He knows the sorrow of His people. Indeed, He is moved with compassion to "come down" personally on behalf of His children. Exodus 3:8 reveals that the Lord our God moves three-fold on behalf of His afflicted people. First, He is moved to deliver us from our afflictions. The bible says that "many are the afflictions of the righteous: but the LORD delivereth him out of them all" (Psalm 34:18-19). Secondly, God is moved to establish his children in a better position. Thirdly, He is moved to bless them with abundant benefits.

Confession: thank you, father, you are my deliverer.

September 25

Ecclesiastes 10-12; 2 Corinthians 11:16-33

Confession

Romans 10:10
For with the heart man believeth unto righteousness; and with the mouth confession is made unto salvation.

Salvation is as easy as this. "Confess with your mouth, "Jesus is Lord," and believe in your heart that God raised him from the dead and you will be saved." What a marvelous thing! So simple, yet so profound. Jesus has done everything for us. Not one thing was left undone by Him. There is nothing left to do except to celebrate this new life offered through the Son of God. It is as simple as that. Being good cannot save you, being baptized cannot save you, and attending church cannot. Only Christ can save you. By confessing this, you trust Him alone to justify you and bring you into fellowship with God. You are placing all your hope in him. This principle is tobe applied to our daily lives. We are to hold onto the promise of God concerning the situation at hand and confess them with thanksgiving until we receive the physical manifestation of our prayers.

Confession: Lord, I receive grace to hold unto your world and confess it daily.

September 26

Song of Solomon 1-3; 2 Corinthians 12

The Lord has given you the land

Joshua 2:9
And she said unto the men, I know that the LORD hath given you the land, and that your terror is fallen upon us, and that all the inhabitants of the land faint because of you.

"I know that the LORD hath given you the land". It is astounding that Rehab the harlot knew that the land had been given to the children of God. And it is equally remarkable that she would turn her back on her people to support Gods children. Indeed, she could have plied her trade to (attempt to) thwart Israel's efforts. But instead, she confesses Israel's God as true and seeks refuge from the spies. As a result, she will be saved, even as her city is destroyed. The lord is still fighting for his children today. God is for us. We don't need to be afraid of what is happening in the world today. The church of God is marching on, and the gates of hail shall not prevail. We, the church, need to encourage people and give them hope in Christ.

Confession: Thank you, Father, for the courage to stand firm in faith at this time.

September 27

Song of Solomon 4-5; 2 Corinthians 13

Don't cry, move on

Exodus 14:15
And the LORD said unto Moses, Wherefore criest thou unto me? speak unto the children of Israel, that they go forward:

What do you do when there is nothing you can do? Where do you go when there is no place you can go? On whom do you depend when there is no one on earth on whom you can rely? On. When we find ourselves in such a situation, we must ask for God's mercy and deliverance. God's battle plans for each of us are drawn to meet our requirements. They are drawn up with regard to our strengths and weaknesses. God never leads us down a road we are unable to walk. Our lack of spiritual maturity may limit what God can and will do for us when encountering personal problems. He will not lead us into a situation that we cannot handle, but he will lead us into situations that will prepare us for deeper waters. We need to ask God to open our eyes to see the lessons we must learn when we find ourselves in such situations.

Confession: Help me, Lord, see the daily lessons you are teaching me.

September 28

Song of Solomon 6-8; Galatians 1

We are sons

Galatians 4:6-7
And because ye are sons, God hath sent forth the Spirit of his Son into your hearts, crying, Abba, Father. Wherefore thou art no more a servant, but a son; and if a son, then an heir of God through Christ.

Christ reveals the fact of the fatherhood of God, but the mere knowledge of that fact which we may derive from studying the words and life of Christ will not enable us to realize the spirit of trustful sonship. It is little to know that God is a Father if we do not experience his fatherhood's love and close relationship. The Spirit of God's firstborn Son is given to the true sons of God. The sonship, Paul teaches, is the consequence of our faith in God as we depend on Him just as children depend on their parents. Therefore, the consciousness of trustful aspiration towards God as our Father is proof of sonship. The Spirit thus bears witness with our spirit that we are sons of God and heir of God through Christ.

Confession: Hallelujah, I am a child of God.

September 29

Isaiah 1-3; Galatians 2

Faith speaks

2 Corinthians 4:13

We having the same spirit of faith, according as it is written, I believed, and therefore have I spoken; we also believe, and therefore speak;

This scripture points out that Paul had a firm commitment to the truth of God's word and the gospel of Christ. He was not going to stop proclaiming the validity of the gospel even if it cost him his life. He was going to preach the gospel that sets men free. He was going to be steadfast in the gospel. A strong faith speaks and stands by the word of God even in adversity. Paul not only has a spirit of faith, a Scripture-based faith, but he also has a settled hope of eternal life with Christ. This should be the hope of all the children of God. And because we have this hope of eternal life, we ought to live by faith. The scripture says that the just shall live by faith. True faith speaks because it sees beyond the physical realm. Are you speaking?

Confession: I believe; therefore, I will keep on speaking the truth of God's word.

September 30

Isaiah 4-6; Galatians 3

Jesus knows all about you

John 2:24-25
But Jesus did not commit himself unto them, because he knew all men, And needed not that any should testify of man: for he knew what was in man.

Jesus knows all about all people. No person is excluded from his knowledge, and no part of our life is excluded. He knows everybody and everything about everybody. You may have succeeded in hiding something all your life from everyone on this earth. But you have not hidden it from Jesus. Therefore, you always have someone to go to for help. The one who knows who you are. One who is always willing to love us unconditionally. One of the great longings of the human soul is to understand ourselves. Who are we? What is our nature? Jesus has the answer to all these questions. He has a special covenant love for those who trust and believe in him. Jesus knows about your fears, your weaknesses, your pain. He is willing to help us always. But are we willing to surrender all to him?

Confession: I surrender all to you, Lord, thank you for your care.

October 1

Isaiah 7-9; Galatians 4

The rough places

Isaiah 40:4

Every valley shall be exalted, and every mountain and hill shall be made low: and the crooked shall be made straight, and the rough places plain.

This is the word of the Lord for his children in this new month. "Every valley shall be exalted, and every mountain and hill shall be made low." Many people have been disappointed in so many ways. Many have had significant property losses through sudden and most unexpected problems. They have been brought down from their comfort to become dependent upon friends and relatives for their daily bread. These disappointments, losses, bereavements are valleys, and the Lord has prepared a way out for those who believe. You may not know how, but he will do it again. But we need to remove every spiritual valley by allowing God to heal our pains and by forgiving people who might have offended us.

Confession: Lord, I believe you will make way for me.

October 2

Isaiah 10-12; Galatians 5

Good gifts

Matthew 7:11
If ye then, being evil, know how to give good gifts unto your children, how much more shall your Father which is in heaven give good things to them that ask him?

What the Lord is saying here is, if a fallen human parent, who has a sin nature is capable of showing love, care, and consideration to their child who asks them for something, how much more will our holy, heavenly Father, who loves us with an everlasting love, bestow His gifts and graces on His blood-bought children? But just as a child trusts his parents to give him good things, so those of us who are God's children must trust our heavenly Father to give good things to us. But sometimes, when the answer seems long in coming, we conclude that God has forgotten us. But I believe that God is working all things together for our good. Elizabeth had to wait so long to have a child because the Child's assignment was to prepare the way for our Lord Jesus Christ.

Confession: I will wait upon God though he tarries I will wait for him.

October 3

Isaiah 13-15; Galatians 6

A stronghold

Nahum 1:7
The Lord is good, a strong hold in the day of trouble; and he knoweth them that trust in him.

Yes, the Lord is good indeed. A songwriter says, "count your blessings, name them one by one, and it will surprise you what the Lord has done." When I look back and see God's goodness and all the prayers He answers, I always remember the scripture that says that God can do exceedingly abundantly above all that we can ask or think (Ephesians 3:20). God is our stronghold. A stronghold is defined as "a place that has been fortified to protect it against attack." The Lord is the one place we can go and confide all our thoughts, fears, hopes, dreams, everything! There is no relationship like the one with our Heavenly Father. God knows all those who trust in Him. Having a personal relationship with our Lord Jesus Christ will truly change your life.

Confession: Thank you, Lord, you are my stronghold in time of trouble.

October 4

Isaiah 16-18; Ephesians 1

You are above all

John 3:31
He that cometh from above is above all: he that is of the earth is earthly, and speaketh of the earth: he that cometh from heaven is above all.

John here affirms that Jesus, our Lord and master is above all. The book of Ephesian 1:20-21 says, "Which he wrought in Christ, when he raised him from the dead, and set him at his own right hand in the heavenly places, Far above all principality, and power, and might, and dominion, and every name that is named, not only in this world but also in that which is to come." Christ is above all principalities and powers, and we are also raised with Christ and sited in heavenly places with him (Ephesian 2:6). So we are above all because we are from above. The knowledge of this truth will help us to mount up with wings as eagles and refuse to be dominated by the enemy's tricks and sachems he brings on our journey to distract us, for we are more than conquerors in Christ Jesus.

Confession: I am above all because I am from above.

October 5

Isaiah 19-21; Ephesians 2

What is idolatry

1 Corinthians 10:14
Wherefore, my dearly beloved, flee from idolatry.

Although God had brought the Israelites out of Egypt, their pagan influence and idolatrous practices were influential in their hearts. And so we find Paul using this Old Testament example of rebellion and idolatry to warn us as believers to flee far from idolatry and paganism. Many Christians are still holding onto ungodly festivals. They even participate by sending money to their earthly parents for these ungodly ceremonies. But other things can become idols in our hearts if we are not watchful. Things like your mobile phone, your Tv, your friends, games and any other thing that takes the place of God in your life. Some people will prefer to be in a friend's party rather than be in the house of God to worship with other believers. Some can be on social media for hours but cannot give one hour to the word of God and prayer. Is anything taking the place of God in your life?

Confession: Lord, let nothing take your place in my life.

October 6

Isaiah 22-23; Ephesians 3

A doer of the work

James 1:25

But whoso looketh into the perfect law of liberty, and continueth therein, he being not a forgetful hearer, but a doer of the work, this man shall be blessed in his deed.

Once we are born again, we are no longer under the Law of sin and death but under the Law of the Spirit of Life in Christ Jesus. But how quickly can we be tempted to view life's problems as being God's fault, instead of taking responsibility, by responding to them in a biblical manner – by taking every issue to Christ and trusting Him to navigate us through the stormy times. We are to look earnestly and continuously at the perfect Law of the Spirit of life, which is ours, by faith, in Christ – and we are to keep on concentrating on Him and focusing on His Word, which sustains us with spiritual strength; guards and protects us from the ravages of the enemy. James reminds us in this verse that. The one who looks intently at the perfect law of liberty and is a doer of the work shall be blessed.

Confession: Lord, I receive grace to be an active doer of your word.

October 7

Isaiah 24-26; Ephesians 4

Examine yourself

2 Corinthians 13:5
Examine yourselves, whether ye be in the faith; prove your own selves. Know ye not your own selves, how that Jesus Christ is in you, except ye be reprobate?

As believers, we are encouraged in this scripture above to examine our hearts to ensure that our faith is founded on Christ and that our witnesses are genuine and not counterfeit. There are several ways that each one of us can examine our own spiritual lives - and perhaps the most important is the witness of the indwelling Holy Spirit with our born-again spirit, as we cry out to the Lord, search me oh God, and know my heart. Examine me and see if any false spirituality lurks within my inner being. We should not focus on the spirituality of others, for only God knows their hearts. Our daily longing should be to know Christ more and abide in him. Our desire is that Christ may live in us so that we may walk in His love.

Confession: Help me, Lord, to examine myself daily.

October 8

Isaiah 27-30; Ephesians 5

Commanded blessing

Deuteronomy 28:8

The Lord shall command the blessing upon thee in thy storehouses, and in all that thou settest thine hand unto; and he shall bless thee in the land which the Lord thy God giveth thee.

This promise was given to the children of Israel on the condition that they harken diligently to the voice of the Lord and do all his commands. This promise is for us today. The Lord has commanded the blessing on those who have made Jesus their Lord and Savior and are living a righteous life. This promise means that whatever you touch, whatever you set your hands on, God will command the blessing upon it, be it a person, thing, or business. So you can touch your children and bless them every day. If you touch your business, it prospers. When you touch a sick person, he gets healed. Jesus paid the price for you to have this blessing. And because Jesus lives in you by His Spirit, what you touch will be blessed too.

Confession: Thank you, father, for blessings us abundantly.

October 9

Isaiah 31-33; Philippians 1

But not abandoned

2 Corinthians 4:8
We are troubled on every side, yet not distressed; we are perplexed, but not in despair.

The enemy seeks to afflict the effective witness of every fruitful disciple. The enemy seeks to crush and perplex our work and witness and desires to hedge us in on every side and press us into depression. He uses whatever method he can to persecute and suppress our walk and bring us to the point of desperation. But greater is He that is in us than he that is in the world, for although we may be afflicted in every way, we are not crushed - for the Lord is our life and our strength. We may be perplexed by all the difficulties we are called upon to face, for His sake. We will not despair because His grace is sufficient for us. His life-giving strength within is perfected in our weakness.

Confession: Thank you, Father, for the innerstrength to overcome challenges.

October 10

Isaiah 34-36; Philippians 2

Who am I

Exodus 3:11
And Moses said unto God, Who am I, that I should go unto Pharaoh, and that I should bring forth the children of Israel out of Egypt?

Here God is giving this charge, this responsibility, this call to Moses to go to Pharaoh and deliver Israelites out of slavery in Egypt. Moses' response is, "Who am I? How could I do this?" Have you ever felt like you can't do what God calls you to do? When Moses says, "Who am I?" God responds basically by saying, "It's not about who you are, it's about who I am. The self-existent God of the universe, and I will be with you". God is with us right now. He lives in us as followers of Christ. So be encouraged today. Your life and all that God has called you to do is not based on who you are. But on who He is, and He is in you to give you everything you need to be who He called you to be and to do things He asked you to do. You just need to trust him.

Confession: Thank you, Father, for giving usall we need to fulfill our divine destiny.

October 11

Isaiah 37-38; Philippians 3

Men ought always to pray

Luke 18:1
And he spake a parable unto them to this end, that men ought always to pray, and not to faint;

In this parable, we are admonished to pray at all times and not to lose heart. We are to take all our worries to God in prayer. Those who trust in Christ alone for needs and necessities and maintain constant communion and uninterrupted fellowship can enjoy God's peace always. A young believer once asked me, "How can I know God more? It is very simple, maintain a close relationship with God. The more you pray and study his word, the more you know about him. Just like couples who love each other would like to spend time together. Your love for God will create a desire in you to spend time with him in prayer and study of his word. Prayer is about fellowshipping with your heavenly father, talking to him, and listening to what he has to say. But many Christians only speak but has no time to be quiet and listen.

Confession: Lord, help me to pray and listen to you.

October 12

Isaiah 39-40; Philippians 4

The advice of the elders

1 Kings 12:8

But he forsook the counsel of the old men, which they had given him, and consulted with the young men that were grown up with him, and which stood before him.

Rehoboam took three days to deliberate upon the People's Bill of Rights and took counsel in that interval. The older men who stood before Solomon advised concession, while the young ones, who had grown up with him, recommended resistance. Wisdom was with the ancients. The interests of a good king should be the happiness of his subjects. So the old men counseled Rehoboam to "serve" the people and "speak good words to them." But Rehoboam, although the son of a wise man, had not the common sense to do so. This shows that wisdom is not inherited. He forsook the older men's counsel and answered the people roughly as the young men advised him. We must choose our counselors wisely and learnwisdom from those ahead of us in life.

Confession: Help me, Lord, to choose my counselors wisely.

October 13

Isaiah 41-42; Colossians 1

The eyes of the Lord

Psalm 33:18-19
Behold, the eye of the Lord is upon them that fear him, upon them that hope in his mercy; To deliver their soul from death, and to keep them alive in famine.

The promises of God are just as sure today as they were when they were recorded in the Bible. But there are instructions we must follow to enjoy these promises. The scripture above says that God's interest is in those who fear him and hope for his mercy. Those who fear the Lord seeks to please him in all things. They place their hope in Jesus Christ; His life, death, and resurrection. With the assurance that Christ has given us victory. We live each moment in this knowledge and then go to bed at night knowing that God is our deliverer and he can provide all our needs according to his riches in glory by Christ Jesus. So no matter what we face in life, God is with us and will protect us. Our faith is the victory that overcomes the world.

Confession: I will walk in fear of the Lord, and I will hope in his mercy.

October 14

Isaiah 43-44; Colossians 2

What has God told you

1 Kings 13:17-18

For it was said to me by the word of the Lord, Thou shalt eat no bread nor drink water there, nor turn again to go by the way that thou camest. He said unto him, I am a prophet also as thou art; and an angel spake unto me by the word of the Lord, saying, Bring him back with thee into thine house, that he may eat bread and drink water. But he lied unto him.

In the passage above, the prophet from Bethel was trying to persuade the man of God from Judah to change his course from doing precisely what God told him. The man of God from Judah listened to the lie from the prophet of Bethel. No matter how natural and seductive this enticement was, it was the duty of the man of God to resist it. He had a word from God to guide his actions and should receive no other word except God's word. His failure at this point ended his usefulness as a man of God. A lion met him on the road and killed him. If something contradicts what God said to you, the lesson here is to go back to God to confirm it.

Confession: Lord, help me do only what you asked me to do.

October 15

Isaiah 45-47; Colossians 3

An angry man

Proverbs 22:24

Make no friendship with an angry man; and with a furious man thou shalt not go:Lest thou learn his ways, and get a snare to thy soul.

Do not make friends with a hot-tempered person, do not associate with one easily angered, or you may learn their ways and get yourself ensnared. We are advised to stay away from angry people and not make them your friends. Anger can lead to sin, especially when control is lost, things are said, and people are hurt. Solomon's advice to us is to stay away from anger. The bible says that anger rests in the bosom of fools. (Ecclesiastes 7:9). The fool lets his feelings take control, and he gives full vent to his anger, caring not who he hits and hurts. On the other hand, the wise person controls his anger, emotions, and feelings. Patience is associated with mercy for others and a belief that God is not finished with them yet, just as He is not finished with us either. We are all a work in progress. Let us be patient with one another.

Confession: Lord, help me to control my feelings. I don't want to be a fool.

October 16

Isaiah 48-49; Colossians 4

Solid food

Hebrews 5:13-14

For every one that useth milk is unskilful in the word of righteousness: for he is a babe. But strong meat belongeth to them that are of full age, even those who by reason of use have their senses exercised to discern both good and evil.

When a baby is born, they are fed with their mother's milk for the first six months of their lives. Then as they grow, they are slowly introduced to solid food. It is natural; one does not have to teach with much effort. The same principle can be used for Christians. At first, they should be gathered and taught the first principles of God's Word. They should be encouraged and led into these amazing truths by those older in Christ. As this happens, their skills should develop for reading and understanding the Word for themselves. Problems arise because we have a multitude of Christians who are not progressing in the natural process of growing up. As believers, we should not remain an infant in the knowledge of the Word.

Confession: Lord, help me grow in knowledge as I spend time in your word daily.

October 17

Isaiah 50-52; 1 Thessalonians 1

An alter for God

Exodus 20:24-25

An altar of earth thou shalt make unto me, and shalt sacrifice thereon thy burnt offerings, and thy peace offerings, thy sheep, and thine oxen: in all places where I record my name I will come unto thee, and I will bless thee. And if thou wilt make me an altar of stone, thou shalt not build it of hewn stone: for if thou lift up thy tool upon it, thou hast polluted it.

The command that Israel was not to contribute to the making of the altar through their craftsmanship or handiwork emphasizes the fact that we cannot contribute to our salvation. We must approach God based solely on what He has done for us on the cross. The point of this instruction and prohibition is this: a man is received into fellowship with God based upon the work of the Lord Jesus Christ, not the merits offered by the man himself. We are saved, not because of our righteous actions but his mercy. The only altar God wants from us is to create an altar of prayer where we can fellowship with him and give him our sacrificial praise.

Confession: I will build an altar of prayer for you, Lord and praise you daily.

October 18

Isaiah 53-55; 1 Thessalonians 2

Fruit needs patience

Luke 8:15
But that on the good ground are they, which in an honest and good heart, having heard the word, keep it, and bring forth fruit with patience.

"Having heard the word, keep it and bring forth fruit with patience" Jesus explains here that for you to bear fruit after giving your life to Jesus, you need patience. We must realize that this seed takes time to bear fruit. Often, we want to produce good fruit in our lives immediately, and we get discouraged when we feel we are falling short. Jesus knows all about our struggles, and he knows that we cannot do it on our own. We have to trust the holy spirit to help us daily. As followers of Jesus, we all have different struggles and vices. Some we can overcome right away, while others may take years or even a lifetime. Be encouraged today that Jesus doesn't expect you to bear all your fruit in one day, but take it day by day, as you put your faith in Him.

Confession: Lord, I receive grace to bring forth fruit with patience.

October 19

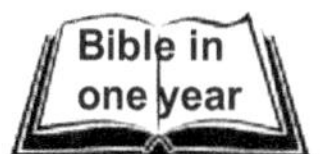

Isaiah 56-58; 1 Thessalonians 3

Evidence of wisdom

James 3:13
Who is a wise man and endued with knowledge among you? let him shew out of a good conversation his works with meekness of wisdom.

Wisdom does not depend on how much knowledge a man manages to acquire but on how a man conducts himself in his everyday life. Godly wisdom is exhibited in the way that a man applies all that he has learned from the Word of God in his daily life and in the decisions and choices he makes. The Lord Jesus is wisdom manifest in human flesh, and He is the living example of a life that is walking in spirit and truth. Jesus is not only the image of the invisible God, but He is also the perfect representation of the way that godly men and god-fearing women should live. The book of Galatians 5:22-23 talks about the fruit of the Spirit, which is the evidence of the wisdom that comes from above, where purity and peace join together in perfect union and where meekness and mercy embrace one another.

Confession: Help me, Lord, to maintain a good conversation always.

October 20

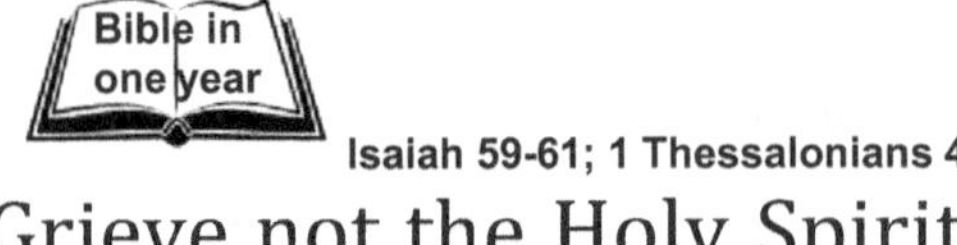

Isaiah 59-61; 1 Thessalonians 4

Grieve not the Holy Spirit

Ephesians 4:30-31
And grieve not the holy Spirit of God, whereby ye are sealed unto the day of redemption.
Let all bitterness, and wrath, and anger, and clamour, and evil speaking, be put away from you, with all malice

The Holy Spirit wants to lead us into a life of victory, the happiest and most fulfilling life a person can ever live. The Bible clarifies that the Holy Spirit and the flesh, our human nature are in total opposition to each other. So I cannot live according to my natural inclinations and at the same time obey the Spirit. We grieve the Holy Spirit by not allowing him to lead us but choosing our way instead. In the scripture above. We need to avoid bitterness, wrath, anger, malice, and evil speaking of one another. These things grieve the Holy Spirit. But the good news is that the Holy Spirit is also the One who gives us the power to obey and overcome all these tendencies in our nature. All he needs is our willingness to obey him.

Confession: Lord, help me put away all the attitudes that grieve the Holy Spirit.

October 21

Isaiah 62-64; 1 Thessalonians 5

God has called you

Acts 13:2
As they ministered to the Lord, and fasted, the Holy Ghost said, Separate me Barnabas and Saul for the work whereunto I have called them.

God wants to use us regardless of our past. Sure, we were sinners before Christ saved us, but we're made into a new creation after we repent and get saved. And now that we're saved, all that God wants us to focus on is His will. In Acts 8, we read that Paul was a terrible persecutor of the church. He persecuted the church to the point that the church continued to fear him (see Acts 9:26). God, however, didn't seem to mind that. Christ personally faced him while he was on his way to persecute more Christians (see Acts 9:1-5). God has called each of us for an assignment. You may be an usher, singer, cleaner, children teacher, or playing an instrument. You will be rewarded based on your faithfulness to what God has called you to do, just like the pastor also will be rewarded if he is faithful.

Confession: Help me, Lord, discover my assignment and be faithful to it.

October 22

Isaiah 65-66; 2 Thessalonians 1

One thing I greatly desire

Psalm 27:4
One thing have I desired of the Lord, that will I seek after; that I may dwell in the house of the Lord all the days of my life, to behold the beauty of the Lord, and to enquire in his temple.

David here expressed one thing he desired of the Lord. One thing which has been the leading object of his life, the thing which he most earnestly desires, is to dwell in the house of the LORD all the days of his life, to behold the beauty of the LORD, and to inquire in his temple. This should also be the desire of every faithful Christian. Though we may be engaged in other things, and though there are other objects of interest in the world, yet our supreme desire on earth should be to dwell always in the presence of God and to be employed in his sacred services here on earth. The service of God upon earth is not burdensome if we trust the Holy Spirit to help us. Spending quality time in His presence strengthens us for the journey ahead.

Confession: Lord, let me dwell in your presence all the days of my life.

October 23

Jeremiah 1-2; 2 Thessalonians 2

Wait for Him

Lamentations 3:25-26
The Lord is good unto them that wait for him, to the soul that seeketh him.
It is good that a man should both hope and quietly wait for the salvation of the Lord.

Jeremiah knew that the secret to a victorious life was to submit to the ways and workings of the Lord – to yield to His testings in life and to surrender to the rod of His chastening - so that like Job we can say, "When He has tried me, I shall come forth as gold" God is good to those that wait for Him – to those that submit to His perfect will and those that trust in His unfailing word. God is good to the person who searches for Him. He is not far from any of us, and He will be found by us - if we search for Him with all our heart. It is good that we hope and quietly wait for the salvation of God. Hope is seeing that there is light despite all of the darkness. Expect only the best from life and take action to get it.

Confession: I will wait for the salvation of the Lord. I shall come forth as gold.

October 24

Jeremiah 3-4; 2 Thessalonians 3

The old paths

Jeremiah 6:16

Thus saith the LORD, Stand ye in the ways, and see, and ask for the old paths, where is the good way, and walk therein, and ye shall find rest for your souls. But they said, We will not walk therein.

The old way isn't the popular way! It is a way that is being abandoned daily by people who have decided that new is better. They leave the true and living God to serve other gods called titles, materialism, degrees, money, and status. The word of God admonished us not to neglect the gathering of believers (Hebrew 10:25). But social media has become an idol and has taken the time we should spend in fellowship with one another. In this text, God is speaking through Prophet Jeremiah to His rebellious and wicked people, who at this time were willfully rebelling against God in their choice of an idolatry lifestyle. This is also happening in the body of Christ today. Many things have become an Idol in our hearts, even our cell phones. God desires that we take the "old way", but it's a choice.

Confession: Thank you, Lord, for leading me to the path that leads to the "old way".

October 25

Jeremiah 5-6; 1 Timothy 1

This is my command

John 15:12-13
This is my commandment, That ye love one another, as I have loved you.
Greater love hath no man than this, that a man lay down his life for his friends.

This command is not something we do if we feel like it. It is to be a deliberate response to another person, regardless of how we feel toward that person. Many think of love as a feeling we have toward another. But God's love, as Jesus speaks of it here, is far deeper than a feeling. This kind of love arises from a deeper relationship with God. Since God is love, love flows from us as we yield to that deeper relationship with God, you will be able to display the qualities of God's love. An expression can be going out of your way to meet a friend's need, having a willingness to spend time with someone in the hospital or prison and being eager to share your food with the hungry. This sacrificial giving pleases God when done from a pure heart.

Confession: Help me, Lord, to deepen my relationship with you so that your love will flow through me to others.

October 26

Jeremiah 7-8; 1 Timothy 2

Complete obedience

2 Corinthians 10:6
And having in a readiness to revenge all disobedience, when your obedience is fulfilled.

When we think through these words of Paul, we see how he simply desired for the children of God to walk in obedience. Jesus Christ wants a disciplined church that obeys Him, and when the church members do, it is to their advantage. Compliance with God and His ways is always most beneficial to those who follow Him. Obedience is the key to enjoying God's blessings. Sometimes we wait on God while He is waiting on us to make our ways right before him. To work on our character, be disciplined, and make restitution where necessary. Especially when the Holy Spirit is laying it to your heart. You may have to ask those ahead in faith for counselling and prayer when you struggle with addiction or issues you don't know how to handle. When your obedience is complete, you will enjoy the blessings of God.

Confession: Help me, Lord, to walk in obedience always.

October 27

Jeremiah 9-10; 1 Timothy 3

For his name's sake

Psalm 23:3

He restoreth my soul: he leadeth me in the paths of righteousness for his name's sake.

David was a man who proved the Lord to be a faithful God, Whose Word was to be trusted. He found the Lord was a God Who kept His promises and whose loving-kindness and great goodness never failed. These beautiful words have not lost any of their profound impact in the difficult days we all face today. Instead, as we meditate on these simple truths, we discover their significance is magnified and multiplied. For it is as we reflect upon these comforting words that we find in them the beloved face of Jesus. 'For his namesake,' This means that God is committed to leading you in the paths of righteousness because you are his child. He is committed to your progress and well-being. Like many beautiful promises throughout Scripture, these beautiful words, which have comforted countless millions of believers, assure us that restoration, guidance, protection, and peace is His promise of love to us all.

Confession: Thank you, Father, for your guidance and restoration.

October 28

Jeremiah 11-13; 1 Timothy 4

On eagles' wings

Exodus 19:4
Ye have seen what I did unto the Egyptians, and how I bare you on eagles' wings, and brought you unto myself.

The children of Israel were brought not only into a state of liberty and honour but into covenant and communion with God. I bore you on eagles' wings. This is the expression of the beautiful tenderness God had shown for them. God not only bare them on the eagle's wing, but he hastened them out. He did it also with great ease, the strength, and swiftness of an eagle: those that faint not, nor are weary, are said to mount up with wings as eagles. Other birds carry their young in their paws, but the eagle has their young upon her wings so that even those archers who shoot cannot hurt their young ones unless they first hit through the old ones. This is what God is doing for those who have taken refuge in him. He will bear us on eagles' wings as we take refuge in him.

Confession: Thank you, Father, for carryingme on eagle wings.

October 29

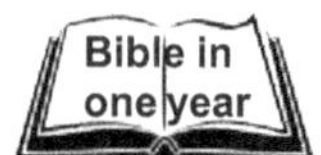

Jeremiah 14-16; 1 Timothy 5

Be good

Galatians 6:10
As we have therefore opportunity, let us do good unto all men, especially unto them who are of the household of faith.

As Christians, we should be known for our goodness. When people hear the word *Christian*, their first thoughts should be integrity, kindness, and good deeds. In our efforts to do good, we must not overlook the priority Paul sets in Galatians 6:10. We are to do good to everyone, but we are to pay special attention to the family of Christ. How we treat our fellow believers is a sign of our faith: "By this everyone will know that you are my disciples if you love one another". Part of doing good to all men is that we don't return evil for evil. Jesus called us to set aside our natural reaction when someone wrongs us. Instead, we are to repay evil with good. We can search for ways we can actively bless people, like, funding hospitals, digging water wells, and meeting the practical needs of people.

Confession: I will use every opportunity to do good by God's grace.

October 30

Jeremiah 17-19; 1 Timothy 6

The favour of God

Matthew 11:29
Take my yoke upon you, and learn of me; for I am meek and lowly in heart: and ye shall find rest unto your souls.

Jesus lived as a man in the way that God desires all His children to live - in lowliness of spirit and complete dependence upon the Father. He lived as man is called to live to demonstrate to us how we should live in utter dependence upon God so that we might know God intimately. The only way to live the Christian life is in total reliance upon the Lord, clinging to Him by faith - admitting our helplessness and trusting in His sufficient strength. And so He calls us to: take My yoke upon you, and learn of Me. The Lord Jesus was meek and lowly in heart, and we are to learn of Him. His entire life was spent living the life of a man that trusted God entirely, and He did only those things that He heard from the Father. In like manner, when we take His yoke upon us and learn to live in continuous dependence upon Him, we too shall find rest for our souls.

Confession: Help me, Lord, learn and live the way you lived while on earth.

October 31

Jeremiah 20-22; 2 Timothy 1

We have an anchor

Hebrews 6:19
Which hope we have as an anchor of the soul, both sure and stedfast, and which entereth into that within the veil.

Our hope in Christ is securely anchored to the Word of God, which contains His will and His purposes so that we are not tossed about by every wind of uncertainty nor destabilized by the stormy and trials of life. We have an anchor that keeps the soul. This anchor is steadfast and sure. It will keep us strong and unmovable in the storms of life. The Bible is God's established and unalterable oath. It is His gracious assurance to those who are His blood-bought children and heirs of the promise. Christ is our great High Priest, and His finished work has established forever that blessed hope set before us in His Word. The hope we have is a sure and steadfast anchor to our soul, and it is a hope that is eternally secure for all who are in Christ Jesus and are holding fast to God's unfailing word.

Confession: I will hold unto the word of God, the anchor that keeps my soul.

November 1

Jeremiah 23-24; 2 Timothy 2

I will restore

Joel 2:25-26
And I will restore to you the years that the locust hath eaten, the cankerworm, and the caterpiller, and the palmerworm, my great army which I sent among you.

When locusts landed on a crop, the destruction went far beyond them, destroying the produce on the land at that time. They also wiped out the seeds saved from the previous year. Therefore, there would be no seeds to be used the following year. They completely ate up all the buds and barks from the trees. Consequently, it would take years for crops to be restored and the land to be redeveloped. But because the people repented and returned to God. God promised His people that He would make up for what had been lost during the four years of the locusts. Have you lost something? Business, marriage, job, or loved one. God can restore lost years by bringing long-term gain from short-term loss and by multiplying your fruitfulness.

Confession: Thank you, father, for this time of restoration.

November 2

Jeremiah 25-26; 2 Timothy 3

Sure foundation

Isaiah 28:16

Therefore thus saith the Lord God, Behold, I lay in Zion for a foundation a stone, a tried stone, a precious corner stone, a sure foundation: he that believeth shall not make haste.

What is this foundation? 1 Peter 2:6 applies this passage directly to the Messiah, Jesus Christ. He is the foundation for our lives, and only with a secure, stable foundation can anything lasting be built. Anything "added on" or not built upon the foundation is sure to end up in ruins. The chief cornerstone carries the weight of the structure. If laid correctly, the weight of the building is evenly distributed, and the structure remains sound. A solid, level foundation is necessary because the wall will eventually fall without that strong base. Christians plan many things and become involved in thousand-and-one good activities, all in the name of Christ and for His kingdom. The problem is that they forget to first consult with the Lord and then wait for His answer and direction. He that believes shall not make haste.

Confession: Lord, you are the sure foundation. I will wait for your direction.

November 3

Jeremiah 27-28; 2 Timothy 4

Proven character

Philippians 2:22
But ye know the proof of him, that, as a son with the father, he hath served with me in the gospel.

What joy Timothy must have been to the apostle Paul. He had learned the holy Scriptures from childhood and was saved by grace through faith - through the ministry of Paul. Timothy lived godly in Christ Jesus, having a desire to see believers grow in grace and knowledge of the Lord Jesus Christ. There is much to learn from this young man. His dedication to the Lord is evident throughout the New Testament. Yet, he had to overcome many difficulties that confronted the early Church. In the same way, we also have to overcome the challenges in Christendom in our times. Christ is sufficient for you, me, and all who seek to please God. We should also seek to walk in the Spirit as we live with one another in the bond of peace.

Confession: Help me, Lord, to live godly and bring others to Christ.

November 4

Jeremiah 29-30; Titus 1

When you satisfy the afflicted

Isaiah 58:10
And if thou draw out thy soul to the hungry, and satisfy the afflicted soul; then shall thy light rise in obscurity, and thy darkness be as the noon day:

From the scripture above, we can see that Injustice, oppression, hunger, homelessness, poverty, nakedness, and slander are God's concerns. They are things that are important and matter to God. And they are not only physical conditions. They can also be emotional and spiritual. We can hunger for a meal, and we can long for love. We can be homeless on the streets and be homeless within ourselves. Nakedness might mean we have no clothes or that we have no hope. God has promised to bless those who will lend a helping hand to the afflicted and give food to the hungry. The truth is that God gives his blessing to be distributed to others. But many people are only concerned about their family alone.

Confession: Help me, Lord, to bless others with my resources.

November 5

Jeremiah 31-32; Titus 2

Be wise as a serpent

Matthew 10:16
Behold, I send you forth as sheep in the midst of wolves: be ye therefore wise as serpents, and harmless as doves.

It is clear that when Jesus says he is sending us as sheep in the midst of wolves, he means that we will be treated the way wolves treat sheep. But Jesus here admonishes us to be wise as a serpent and harmless as doves. The serpent intelligence and the dove's innocence are designed to keep the sheep out of trouble. We can go among wolves and be vulnerable as we preach the gospel, but we should step aside when they lunge at us. We are also advised to be as innocent as doves. That is, don't give them any legitimate reason to accuse you of injustice or immorality. Keep your reputation as clean as you can. Do not allow the wicked to speak against God. Let the wisdom of God guide you always.

Confession: Help me, Lord, be wise as a serpent and harmless as a dove.

November 6

Jeremiah 33-35; Titus 3

Do not compare

2 Corinthians 10:12
For we dare not make ourselves of the number, or compare ourselves with some that commend themselves: but they measuring themselves by themselves, and comparing themselves among themselves, are not wise.

Each of us lives under a unique set of circumstances. We are working on different problems, growing on diverse character traits at various rates. We experience trials and have been influenced by our environment differently. A true and accurate comparison is impossible by another human being. It misses the mark of perfection according to the truth of God. Only God can truly judge a person, for only He can judge the heart and observe the entire picture. God's righteous judgment is based on truth. This means that His decisions are reached based on reality, on the facts of the case, not on appearances or intentions. It also means He judges without partiality to rank or wealth. Finally, it means that He judges against an authoritative and unchanging standard.

Confession: Help me, Lord, appreciate where I am now without comparing with others.

November 7

Jeremiah 36-37; Philemon

His ears are open

Psalm 34:15
The eyes of the Lord are upon the righteous, and his ears are open unto their cry.

God is attentive to the cries of the righteous. Just as a parent listens to the cries of a child in pain or need, God hears and helps his children who are in need. God loves us in a way that is so far beyond what human parents can do. Our parents helped us in time of need. We can be assured that God not only listens but has planned a response already for our cries. However, God's answer may be delayed for various reasons. Demonic activity may impede response to prayer, like the case of Daniel (Daniel 10:1-14). God may also be waiting for the necessary spiritual development before the answer is provided. Whatever the reason, God has already provided the answer. Be patient for its arrival and take time to intensify in prayers. God will never come late.

Confession: Thank you, Lord, for answering all our prayers in your way.

November 8

Jeremiah 38-39; Hebrews 1

More grace

James 4:6
But he giveth more grace. Wherefore he saith, God resisteth the proud, but giveth grace unto the humble.

From the beginning of Genesis to the final Revelation of Jesus Christ, we discover that God opposes the proud but favours the humble. He resists arrogance but gives grace to those lowly of heart. The evils of the world are conceived and birthed through the corruption of our hearts and the lusts of our flesh. James reminds us that God gives us grace and even greater grace. He also urges us not to abuse His mercies by imitating the world's ways, which is at enmity with God – but rather to walk in spirit and truth. Knowing that grace is given to the humble, we should earnestly seek after the precious fruit of the Spirit, which will only develop and grow in the one that recognizes that every manifestation of sin is rooted in a proud and arrogant heart - but He gives grace to the humble.

Confession: Help me, Lord, to be humble.

November 9

Jeremiah 40-42; Hebrews 2

The just shall live by faith

Hebrews 10:38-39
Now the just shall live by faith: but if any man draw back, my soul shall have no pleasure in him. But we are not of them who draw back unto perdition; but of them that believe to the saving of the soul.

As Christians, we are called to live the life of faith. We are to run the race of faith and not be weary; we are to walk by faith and not by sight. And the way to achieve this is by faith - not by works of the Law. It is by walking in spirit and truth through the power of the indwelling Spirit of Christ and not relying on our limited human abilities. God takes no pleasure in his born-again children living a life of unbelief. Because He has clothed us in the righteousness of Christ, sent the Holy Spirit to live in us, and given us the Word of God, we have no excuse for drawing back into unbelief or fearfulness. The just shall live by faith.

Confession: I will please God by walking in faith.

November 10

Jeremiah 43-45; Hebrews 3

Abide in his love

John 15:9
As the Father hath loved me, so have I loved you: continue ye in my love.

The love about which the Lord Jesus was speaking was not the ordinary love that flows from the heart of a human soul. He was not speaking of a mother's love for her newborn, a husband's love for his bride, or a patriot's love for his country. The reciprocated love of the Father and the Son is unfathomable in human terms, for it has no beginning and will never end. It spans from eternity past into the eternal ages to come. We are surrounded by our human love which can fluctuate often. Human love can grow cold, relationships become tired, and affection can subside as circumstances change. Yet the deep and incredible love the Father has for His Son is the same deep and great love that Jesus has for His people - for you and me. He made a point of telling His disciples that His love for them is as passionate glorious, and eternal as the love that flows between Him and His Father.

Confession: Thank you, Jesus, for loving me so much.

November 11

Jeremiah 46-48; Hebrews 4

Measure of faith

Romans 12:3
For I say, through the grace given unto me, to every man that is among you, not to think of himself more highly than he ought to think; but to think soberly, according as God hath dealt to every man the measure of faith.

God has given us all that we need for life and godliness because we trusted in Christ's finished work by faith. By His Word and through His Spirit, we have received all that we require, including certain spiritual gifts, so that we may live a life that honours His name. Each of us has been blessed by God with certain spiritual gifts, and we are to exercise those gifts according to the measure of faith and the grace we receive from God. We should neither exaggerate nor minimize the gifts we received from above - but should do everything to the glory of God. All spiritual gifts are given by grace and exercised by faith. We are saved by faith, we are to live by faith, and we are to exercise our spiritual gifts by faith - and all is to be done to the glory of God and not for the elevation of self.

Confession: Lord, I receive grace to do everything to your glory.

November 12

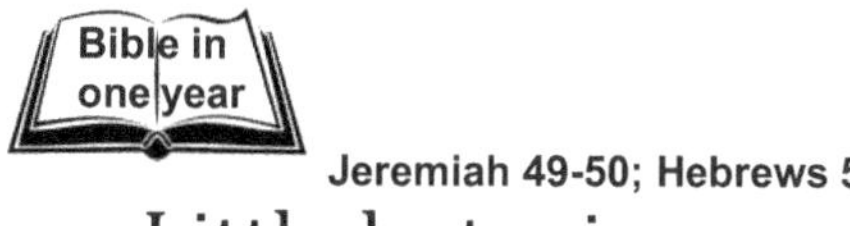

Jeremiah 49-50; Hebrews 5

Little but wise

Proverbs 30:28
The spider taketh hold with her hands, and is in kings' palaces.

This spider that Solomon saw on the wall might have said: "I can't weave a web worthy of this great palace; what can I do amid all this gold and embroidery? I am not able to make anything fit for so great a place, and so I will not work my spinning jenny." Not so said the spider. "The spider taketh hold with her hands." Oh, what a lesson that is for you and me! What if the spider of the text refuses to move its shuttle because it cannot weave Solomon's robe? The truth is that If you are lazy with one talent, you would be lazy with ten talents too. What God does, He does well. What you do, do well, be it great or small work. If ten talents, employ all the ten. If five talents, use all the five; if one talent, employ the one. There is an order for promotion in the Lord's army, but you cannot be a general until you have been a captain, a lieutenant, and a colonel. It is step-by-step.

Confession: Help me, Lord, to be faithful in little beginning.

November 13

Jeremiah 51-52; Hebrews 6

According to ability

Matthew 25:15
And unto one he gave five talents, to another two, and to another one; to every man according to his several ability; and straightway took his journey.

We can see in the passage above that the master gives to each servant talents, "...each according to their ability." The master understood that the one-talent servant could not produce as much as the five-talent servant. Even though we're not created equal in regard to the talents we're given, there is equality found in the Parable of the Talents. It comes from the fact that it takes just as much work for the five-talent servant to produce five more talents as it does for the two-talent servant to produce two more talents. This is why the reward given by the master is the same. The master measures success by degrees of effort, as should be. This parable also teaches us that we work for the Master, not for selfish purposes. And we will be held accountable for how we use our work to fulfil our earthly callings.

Confession: Thank you, father, for the talents. I will use them for your glory.

November 14

Lamentations 1-2; Hebrews 7

Practice what you learn

Philippians 4:9
Those things, which ye have both learned, and received, and heard, and seen in me, do: and the God of peace shall be with you.

Paul himself was profoundly aware of his God-appointed role. He knew, of course, that he wasn't an example of how to be a perfect man. He had formerly been a vicious antagonist against Jesus Christ and a notorious persecutor of the church. But, by the grace of God, he became the chief example of what it looks like for a sinner to be saved by faith in Jesus Christ and to rise then and walk in fellowship with the Savior. We could go on and on and on—talking about Paul's example of devotion to the Scripture. His faithfulness in prayer, his preaching in the face of danger, and his sacrifice in service to God's people. But in learning all these things that Paul's example sets before us, we must take them out of the realm of theory and put them into the realm of practice. As he stresses, we must "do" them.

Confession: Help me, Lord, practice what you teach me daily.

November 15

Lamentations 3-5; Hebrews 8

He will not fail thee

Deuteronomy 31:8
And the Lord, he it is that doth go before thee; he will be with thee, he will not fail thee, neither forsake thee: fear not, neither be dismayed.

What an encouraging promise Moses gave to Joshua and all Israel. And this is a promise from the Lord, which is equally true for Christians in today's Church dispensation, as it was for the nation of Israel during the dispensation of Law. The Lord had promised to go before us, just as He promised Israel. He has promised to be with us always - even to the end of the age. What a comfort to know that He will never fail us nor forsake us. God's Word is to be trusted. He has promised to go before us, to lead us and prepare the way we take, even when we let Him down. He has promised to be with us on our journey through life and to stay with us through all the circumstances of life - even during those times when we prove faithless. God has promised never to leave us alone.

Confession: Thank you, Lord, you will never fail me.

November 16

Ezekiel 1-3; Hebrews 9

Don't be troubled

John 14:1
Let not your heart be troubled: ye believe in God, believe also in me.

The central message in Jesus' words above is that the basis of comfort in any situation we find ourselves in is simple, trusting faith. If you're discontent, worried or anxious, the reason is that you don't trust Him as you should. If you trust Christ, what do you have to worry about? In John 20:29, after Jesus showed Thomas the nail prints in His hands, He said, "Because you have seen Me, have you believed? Blessed are they who did not see and yet believed." He was trying to get across that His visible presence was not nearly as significant as an understanding of His spiritual presence. He is there, labouring on our behalf, even when we cannot see Him. "Lo, I am with you always, even to the end of the age" (Matthew 28:20).

Confession: Lord, I believe you have answered, even though I have not seen the physical manifestation.

November 17

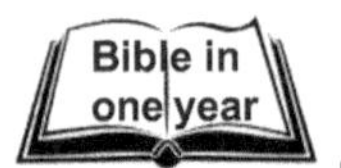

Ezekiel 4-6; Hebrews 10:1-23

Peculiar treasure

Exodus 19:5
Now therefore, if ye will obey my voice indeed, and keep my covenant, then ye shall be a peculiar treasure unto me above all people: for all the earth is mine

To be a peculiar treasure means that You're unique and special to God, the most cherished and celebrated of all His creation. God chose you to be the one to show forth His praises and manifest his glory on earth. You're a special person. But for you to bring out the treasures within, you have to obey the voice of your heavenly father. When you were born again, you became an obedient child of God, and as a result, you became a peculiar treasure unto God. And as you continue in obedience to his voice, your life will show forth his glory. We should live with the consciousness that we're not ordinary people; we're a peculiar treasure to God! That's why He paid such a high price, the blood of His Son Jesus, to redeem us. Every day, we should hold our heads up with dignity and say, "I'm unique to God; I'm His peculiar treasure.

Confession: I am Gods peculiar treasure; I am unique to God.

November 18

Ezekiel 10-12; Hebrews 11

Labour to enter his rest

Hebrews 4:11
Let us labour therefore to enter into that rest, lest any man fall after the same example of unbelief.

Because of disobedience and unbelief, the children of Israel did not enter into the rest that God had promised them. They treated the promises of God with disdain and paid little heed to His Word. And many of us Christians are doing the same today. They disobeyed God by working in unbelief. The scripture above shows us how to enter into the rest that God has for us. It is by labouring in the word of God, and meditating in his promises because faith comes by hearing the word of God. The rest we are exhorted to enter is a rest we can experience today. Christ is our rest, and we are called to give diligence to enter into that rest - today. The peace of God will guide our hearts and minds in Christ Jesus if we abide in Him, rest in Him, submit to Him -and believe in his promises.

Confession: I will labour in the word of God to enter his rest.

November 19

Ezekiel 13-16; Hebrews 12

In my name

Mark 16:17
And these signs shall follow them that believe; In my name shall they cast out devils; they shall speak with new tongues.

The name of Jesus is mighty. There is no other name that you can place at The same strata as you place the name of Jesus. That's why the Bible says that "God has given him a name which is above every other name." It is the most important name. The name of Jesus includes all that you will ever need in this life and in the life to come. Not only is it the most important name and the most inclusive name, but it is the most irresistible name. Let's look at three things the name of Jesus can do. It has the power to save. Romans 10:13 says, "Whosoever shall call upon the name of the Lord shall be saved." the name of Jesus has the power to spoil the works of Satan, just as the scripture above says. The name of Jesus has the power to supply. In Philippians 4:19, the apostle Paul said, "But my God shall supply all your need according to his riches in glory by Christ Jesus."

Confession: Thank you, Jesus, you are the sweetest name I know.

November 20

Ezekiel 17-20; Hebrews 13

They looked unto Him

Psalm 34:5
They looked unto him, and were lightened: and their faces were not ashamed.

Looking unto the Lord is an attitude of the soul, an act of the will, and the exercise of faith, a turning away from all that is of the world and relying solely upon the living God. When you focus your eyes on God, the light will come. The wisdom you need for the issue at hand will be delivered to you. Those that look upon the Lord place no reliance upon self, have no confidence in the flesh. Their hearts are engaged with almighty God, and, like Moses, they endure "as seeing him who is invisible" (Heb 11:27). This characterizes those who are members of the Household of Faith: in their need, they look to God for their supplies. In their straits, they look to God for deliverance. In their trouble, they look to God for comfort. In their weakness, they look to God for strength. This distinguishes the children of God from unbelievers, who lean upon the "arm of flesh" and look to their fellows for help.

Confession: Thank you, Jesus, I will not be ashamed because I look unto you.

November 21

Ezekiel 21-23; James 1

Pleasing sacrifice

Hebrews 13:6
So that we may boldly say, The Lord is my helper, and I will not fear what man shall do unto me.

The character of the Lord Jesus and attributes of God are changeless: they're unalterable; immutable; indestructible; irrevocable, and lasting, and one by one, scripture has unveiled the unchangeable nature of God. And step-by-step the book of Hebrews demonstrates the difference between a life of trusting faith and one that lives in doubting unbelief.
If only our faith were simpler, and we were more childlike, we would take all that God says in the Scriptures, and we would trust in His Word – and that's called FAITH!! Faith is just having confidence, is what God says. Faith is also an action. You cannot sit at home all day when looking for a job. You need to write an application to various companies. God is our helper, but we need to do our part too. There is something you do while you are waiting for the manifestation of your dreams.

Confession: Help me, Lord, to take the necessary action to actualize my dreams.

November 22

Ezekiel 24-26; James 2-3

His grace is not in vain

1 Corinthians 15:10
But by the grace of God I am what I am: and his grace which was bestowed upon me was not in vain; but I laboured more abundantly than they all: yet not I, but the grace of God which was with me.

What Paul says here is that everything he is is totally by God's grace. God's grace has made me who I am. God's grace has saved me. Grace is the undeserved favour God demonstrated in the sacrificial death of Christ. Christ's death is the reason why people can freely enter into salvation and a relationship with God. This grace received in salvation must not be accepted in vain, meaning "without content, empty, without result, or useless," but is to be taken as stewardship. God has called us to be ambassadors for Christ and given us the ministry of reconciling the world to Him. Not to do so is to receive the grace which saved us in vain or not to benefit all the lost souls around us. Paul engaged the grace of God upon his life, and he laboured in the work of God and brought souls to Christ.

Confession: Lord, your grace upon my life will not be in vain in Jesus name.

November 23

Ezekiel 27-28; James 4

Time to flee

2 Timothy 2:22
Flee also youthful lusts: but follow righteousness, faith, charity, peace, with them that call on the Lord out of a pure heart.

All kinds of different "youthful" lusts can plague people who remain immature in thinking, even if they are well along in their years as Christians. The lust for pleasure. Thisincludes uncontrolled sexual obsession, but it doesn't stop with sex. There may be an obsession with drinking, drugs, eating, and many other things. There are all kinds of different "youthful" lusts. The Lust for power. The Lust for the material things. Paul's advice to Timothy is simple: Run! Run from these things. Guard against being controlled by a video game, drugs or anything else that grabs hold of you. But instead, be controlled by the Holy Spirit. Listen and obey that gentle voice within you. When we give in to excesses, We put ourselves in positions where we will make mistakes that we will have to live with for a lifetime.

Confession: Help me, Lord, to flee from lust and be controlled by the Holy Spirit.

November 24

Ezekiel 29-31; James 5

Unbelieving believer

Matthew 21:22
And all things, whatsoever ye shall ask in prayer, believing, ye shall receive.

We must remember that prayer isn't simply a means of asking for things but rather an opportunity to fellowship with our heavenly father. The goal of prayer is to talk to God and for Him to respond through His Word and the voice of the Holy Spirit. We submit our desires and supplications, our thanksgiving and praise to God, and He molds our hearts to desire and agree with his will. This happens when we get to the place where our heart cries, "Not my will but yours be done" *That's* how we will match up. All things you ask in prayer must be his will. Healing, long life, progress and abundant life are all Gods will. But you have to seek his face to know the assignment he has for you and the place of the assignment. Prayer isn't about begging God to change His mind to come around to our side of thinking; it's about God changing our hearts and minds to come around to His. Then our desires and requests are part of His will.

Confession: Lord, let me desire only what you want for my life.

November 25

Ezekiel 32-33; 1 Peter 1

Persecuted but not forsaken

2 Corinthians 4:8
We are hard-pressed on every side, yet not crushed; we are perplexed, but not in despair;

The word "pressed" was sometimes used for walking through a crowd were people surrounded you and pressed against you. "We are pressed on every side by troubles, but we are not crushed". "We catch it from every direction, but we don't let them squeeze the life out of us". Sometimes we just don't know which way to go. Life has a way of throwing us a curveball now and then. Sometimes we face such confusing circumstances that we honestly don't know what we need or want or the best thing to do. Paul himself said in Romans 8:26 that sometimes we don't know how to pray. We can just ask for God's mercy and pray in tongues, trusting the Holy Spirit for help at such moments. But in all these things, the power of Christ is there to help us through trouble.

Confession: Thank you father, though we may be hard-pressed, you are there to help us.

.

November 26

Ezekiel 34-35; 1 Peter 2

There is hope

Ecclesiastes 9:4-5

For to him that is joined to all the living there is hope: for a living dog is better than a dead lion. For the living know that they shall die: but the dead know not anything, neither have they any more a reward; for the memory of them is forgotten.

"For a living dog is better than a dead lion". It is said that "when there is life, there is hope". The New Testament idea of hope differs from our usual thinking about hope. In the New Testament sense, we can define hope as a full assurance or strong confidence that God will do good to us in the future. But there is something even more peculiar about Christian hope: Peter calls it "living hope."(I Peter 1:3). Living hope is hope that has power and produces changes in life. "living hope" is fertile, fruitful and productive. Christian hope arises in the heart through hearing a credible testimony to the resurrection of Jesus Christ from the dead. And because Jesus lives, we can face tomorrow with confidence.

Confession: Thank you, Jesus, because you live, I can face tomorrow.

November 27

Ezekiel 36-37; 1 Peter 3

True worshipers

John 4:24
God is a Spirit: and they that worship him must worship him in spirit and in truth.

When we are born again, we become one spirit with God's Spirit, and we become partakers of the divine nature: The fact that God is spirit demands that we worship him in spirit and truth. To worship in spirit is to worship from our heart or inner being. Jesus spoke of people who honored God with their lips, but their hearts were far away from Him (Matthew 15:8). To worship in spirit is to worship with "complete sincerity," and to worship in truth is to worship in "complete reality." Jesus gave the key when He said: "*I am the way, the TRUTH, and the Life*" (John 14:6). There is no truth in the Devil, who is "a liar and the father of lies" (John 8:44). Even now the Devil sows lies to distract us from the worship of the true God.

Confession: I will worship you the true God in complete sincerity and reality in Jesus' name.

November 28

Ezekiel 38-39; 1 Peter 4

I will arise

Luke 15:17-18
And when he came to himself, he said, How many hired servants of my father's have bread enough and to spare, and I perish with hunger! I will arise and go to my father, and will say unto him, Father, I have sinned against heaven, and before thee.

"And when he came to himself", we are made by God in the image of God for God. These are the three main things about your identity as a human being. You are created by God, like God, and for God. Therefore, conversion is "coming to yourself" and coming to God. It is discovering your identity. You can't know yourself or relate properly to yourself if you are running from the one who made you for himself. God made you in His image. What will you find when you turn home to God through Jesus Christ? In verse 22 of our text, "The father said to his slaves, 'Quickly bring out the best robe and put it on him and put a ring on his hand and sandals on his feet.'" This is how God welcomes us home. He puts on us His robe of righteousness.

Confession: Thank you, Father, for your love, I return to you.

November 29

Ezekiel 40; 1 Peter 5

Christ in you

Colossians 1:27
To whom God would make known what is the riches of the glory of this mystery among the Gentiles; which is Christ in you, the hope of glory.

We are positioned IN Christ and seated with Him in heavenly places at salvation. At salvation, we become a new creation In Christ, and He gives us His life, a newborn-again life. At redemption, we receive the same eternal life of Jesus Christ, who rose from the dead in power and great glory and triumphed over Satan, sin, and death. At salvation, we were imputed with Christ's righteousness so that IN Him and THROUGH Him and BY Him and FOR Him we have power over sin, Satan, and our old, fleshly Adamic nature. The excellent mystery given to us through Paul, which was hidden in ages past, is Christ in you; Christ in me; Christ in us; Christ in every member of the body of believers - Christ in you the hope of glory. This is a glorious truth.

Confession: Thank you, Jesus, for living in me. You are the hope of glory.

November 30

Ezekiel 41-42; 2 Peter 1

When you praise him

Psalm 67:5-6
Let the people praise thee, O God; let all the people praise thee.Then shall the earth yield her increase; and God, even our own God, shall bless us.

Living a life of praise is not only the most enjoyable way to live, but it's also one of the most powerful ways to change your life. Praise is not what you do when good things happen. But it's more like the engine of a train that makes things happen. It will bring an increase in every area of your life. Praise affects you, and it affects God. It touches everything and every part of your life. Likewise, a lack of praise negatively affects you and doesn't bless God. We may not feel joyful, but Scripture tells us in Galatians 5:22 that the fruit of the Spirit is joy. If we have the Holy Spirit, we have joy. We may not feel that joy, but we can choose to lift our hands and speak forth praise to God by faith. Learning to praise God even when everything is going badly will change our hearts, make us much more effective, and cause our faith to abound.

Confession: I receive grace to praise you in all situations.

December 1

Ezekiel 43-44; 2 Peter 2

They spoiled the Egyptians

Exodus 12:36
And the Lord gave the people favour in the sight of the Egyptians, so that they lent unto them such things as they required. And they spoiled the Egyptians.

This is considered a form of payment for allthe years the Hebrews had spent in slavery. This incident provides a wonderful example of the mysterious ways of the providence of Almighty God. God has a way of compensating his children who have been deprived of their rights. Sometimes you may be denied your promotion because of the wicked, and you don't have anybody to speak for you. Hear what God is saying to you in Exodus 14:14 ." The Lord shall fight for you, and ye shall hold your peace." God will collect back all that belongs to you that the enemy is sitting upon just as he did for the Israelites. God will see that all things turn around for your good. The favour of God will speak for you. You just need to hold your peace and allow God to have faith in you.

Confession: Thank you, father, for fighting for me.

December 2

Ezekiel 45-46; 2 Peter 3

Present your body

Romans 12:1
I beseech you therefore, brethren, by the mercies of God, that ye present your bodies a living sacrifice, holy, acceptable unto God, which is your reasonable service.

God is already committed to those of us who are in Christ. When we live our lives in service to God, we are simply returning love and respect to the one who has already given us everything. "How do I live my life as an offering or service to God?" As with all biblical commands, we should begin with the attitude of our hearts. Without the right motives, our good deeds mean nothing to God. Paul tells us how in verse 2 of the text above. First, We are to reject things in the world that do not line up with Scripture. We are to be inwardly transformed and renewed, which will work its way out into actions. We should be able to discern the will of God. By complying with these instructions, we present our bodies as a living sacrifice to God.

Confession: Help me, Lord, to be a living sacrifice by walking in obedience to you.

December 3

Ezekiel 47-48; 1 John 1

The Lord gave Job twice

Job 42:10
And the Lord turned the captivity of Job, when he prayed for his friends: also the Lord gave Job twice as much as he had before.

Comfort in the troubles of life is not only to have circumstances fixed or changed but to experience love understanding and sympathy from friends and family. Job's final test was to pray for his three friends who had persecuted and slandered him and were miserable comforters. His natural heart would never be able to forgive these men for their merciless treatment. But he humbled himself, prayed for them, and forgave them. And, after he has prayed for his friends, God begins to restore him in other areas. Knowing God's grace towards him, Job extends grace and forgiveness to his friends. This is one of the best ways to experience restoration. What is outstanding here is that God gave him double what he had before. Besides restoring friendships and fortunes, God also restored to Job, his family.

Confession: Lord, I receive grace to pray for those who offend me.

December 4

Daniel 1-2; 1 John 2

Be an example

1Timothy 4:12
Let no man despise thy youth; but be thou an example of the believers, in word, in conversation, in charity, in spirit, in faith, in purity.

Although we are unable to control the attitude of others towards ourselves, Paul helped to equip Timothy to deal with this situation in a most biblical manner. None of us can prevent another person from despising or expressing contempt towards us. Still, we are to be responsible for how we react to any hostile attitude others may show towards us. And Paul's advice to Timothy was, "Don't let anyone despise you – but if they do, make sure that in speech, conduct, love, faith, and purity, you show yourself to be an example of a godly believer". People react and respond to issues and words based on their level of growth and their upbringing. But as believers, we should be an example. That is why we are called the light of the world. We are to respond to people based on this knowledge and trust the Holy Spirit to help us.

Confession: Help me, Lord, to be an example of a true believer.

December 5

Daniel 3-4; 1 John 3

God has a plan

Jeremiah 29:11
For I know the thoughts that I think toward you, saith the Lord, thoughts of peace, and not of evil, to give you an expected end.

God's plan isn't always what we thought it would be. But God's plan is always best, even if we don't understand it at the time. We know, though, that in all things, God works together for the good of those who love Him. (Romans 8:28) We know that when one door is shut, God opens another. We know that God is working through every event in our lives to make us more and more dependent on Him for everything we need. We need to realise that God's plan is not always the easiest in our eyes, but it is always the best. The Lord knows the plans He has for us, and He is patiently waiting for us to come to Him. Our prayer life, worship habits, and personal devotion are crucial in every Christian's life because battles are won in prayer, sin is conquered in prayer, discouragement is defeated in prayer, and God is exalted in prayer.

Confession: Thank you, Father, for the excellent plan you have for me.

December 6

Daniel 5-6; 1 John 4

Hold fast

Hebrews 4:15
For we have not an high priest which cannot be touched with the feeling of our infirmities; but was in all points tempted like as we are, yet without sin.

We truly can say that we DO have a great High Priest Who understands ALL our weaknesses, for He faced the same testing that we do, but He did not sin – and He is with us today and lives inside us as we face our own troubles and trials. Although our great High Priest is the eternal Son of God, He laid aside His glory and became the incarnate Word of God so that as the perfect Son of Man, He could identify with the human race in every way– for He was tempted like as we are yet He did not sin. He was poor, yet He trusted God for all His needs. He was despised and rejected by men and yet did not retaliate, but instead handed everything over to the Father. He was falsely accused, yet He opened not His mouth, for He trusted God to vindicate Him. Jesus is the only one who understands how we feel in every situation.

Confession: Thank you, Jesus, for your comfort in difficult times.

December 7

Daniel 7-8; 1 John 5

For your sake

2 Corinthians 8:9
For ye know the grace of our Lord Jesus Christ, that, though he was rich, yet for your sakes he became poor, that ye through his poverty might be rich.

Our minds cannot conceive of the infinite riches of the eternal Son of God, Jesus Christ. For though He was rich beyond all measure, yet for our sake, He became poor, so that by His poverty He could make us rich beyond our wildest imagination. All things were made by Him, and all things were made for Him. All these unimaginable riches and the glories of His elevated heavenly status were laid aside simply because of His GRACE towards us. Though He was the Creator of the universe, He was born into a human race that had rebelled against their creator - He came into a fallen world that was in bondage to the evil governance of Satan. The Son of God did all this for love of you and love of me - so that by His deep poverty, we might become rich.

Confession: Thank you, Jesus, for your grace and love towards me.

December 8

Daniel 9-10; 2 John

The Lord of harvest

Matthew 9:37-38
Then saith he unto his disciples, The harvest truly is plenteous, but the labourers are few; Pray ye therefore the Lord of the harvest, that he will send forth labourers into his harvest.

"Ask the Lord of the harvest, therefore, to send out workers into his harvest field". Jesus is overwhelmed by his love for people as he sees the vastness of the crowds, the perplexity of their problems, and the sense of urgency in reaching them. The religious leaders of Jesus' day saw the ordinary people as trash to be destroyed and burned up. But Jesus saw them as a harvest to be reaped and saved. The harvest will never be reaped unless there are reapers to reap it. Jesus' followers today need to see people as Jesus saw them - as plentiful, precious, perplexed, and perishing. We can take responsibility for our field. Think of all the people we contact every day: family, friends, neighbors, work associates, the woman at the cleaners, the guy at the car wash; that is our field. We are responsible for them.

Confession: Help me, Lord, to bring souls into your kingdom.

December 9

Daniel 11-12; 3 John

Let your heart pant after God

Psalm 42:1
As the hart panteth after the water brooks, so panteth my soul after thee, O God.

It is the very core of our being, the entire person, the innermost self that aches for God with a deep, deep thirst that cries out to the Lord for help. It is then that we come to the end of ourselves and realise that the broken cisterns of this aggressive world can never provide what we need. It is the man or woman who has exhausted their human strength that gasps for the still pools of deep refreshment that no one but the Good Shepherd of the sheep provides for all those who are His. God alone is the only One that can satiate our hunger and satisfy our thirsty souls. He alone can protect our hearts and minds from the deep deception that is coming on the earth and help our fainting souls. Let us go before him every day and allow Him to fill our thirsty souls as we fellowship with him and remain stillin his presence to hear what He has for us.

Confession: Lord, let my heart long for you always.

December 10

Hosea 1-4; Jude

Our deliverer

Psalm 34:19
Many are the afflictions of the righteous: but the Lord delivereth him out of them all.

Affliction is "a state of pain, distress, grief or misery; a cause of mental or bodily pain, as sickness, loss, calamity, or persecution." David was familiar with trying times and difficult circumstances. He always trusted God for deliverance. Although both the righteous and the wicked have troubles, the outcome of their circumstances is different because of their different relationships with the Lord. God knows and sees everything and is concerned for the good of those who love Him. Even in our weakest moments, when our anguish and affliction is too much to bear, Jesus meets us in our suffering on a personal level. God faithfully delivers us, sometimes carrying us through each storm, valley, depression, addiction, and dark season. The joy and peace we have in Him sustain us through every trial, supernaturally.

Confession: Thank you, father, for delivering me from all afflictions.

December 11

Hosea 5-8; Revelation 1

Work out your salvation

Philippians 2:12

Wherefore, my beloved, as ye have always obeyed, not as in my presence only, but now much more in my absence, work out your own salvation with fear and trembling.

The command is for believers to make a continuing, sustained effort to work out to ultimate completion their salvation, which has been graciously granted to them by God through their faith in Jesus Chris. The principle of working out salvation has two aspects. The first pertains to personal conduct, to faithful, obedient daily living. Such obedience involves active commitment and individual effort. For example, you need to search out the scriptures on healing and meditate on them daily until there is an entrance. So also in all issues of life. The second aspect of working out one's salvation is the perseverance of faithful obedience to the end. It is those who remain faithful to the end that receives the crown of glory.

Confession: Help me, Lord, to work out my salvation and remain faithful to the end.

December 12

Hosea 9-11; Revelation 2

Continual praise

Hebrews 13:15
By him therefore let us offer the sacrifice of praise to God continually, that is, the fruit of our lips giving thanks to his name.

Praise is often our response to some action that directly benefits us, and we feel generous because we extend it. We often find it easy to praise God from the same motivation. When He has blessed us, helped us, and protected us. But there are those times when God did not come through the way we thought He would. The medical test comes back positive, The spouse wants a divorce, or a child is wayward. To praise God in those times requires personal sacrifice. It takes an act of the will to lay our all on the altar before God. When we bring a "sacrifice of praise," we choose to believe that, even though life is not going as we think it should, God is still good and can be trusted. Sacrificial praise provokes God's divine intervention because he inhabits the praises of his children (Psalm 22:3).

Confession: I will offer you the sacrifice of praise,Lord, because you can be trusted.

December 13

Hosea 12-14; Revelation 3

I see the invisible

Hebrews 11:27
By faith he forsook Egypt, not fearing the wrath of the king: for he endured, as seeing him who is invisible.

It was by faith that Moses endured as seeing Him who is invisible. What an incredible statement. From his earliest days, Moses saw faith modeled in the lives of his parents. They did not know whether they would live or die, but they lived their lives looking to the invisible God for grace and strength. Parents need to show children how to live, by seeing Him who is invisible. Sometimes it may seem you are doing your best to model that kind of faith, but you are not getting through. It often takes a while for the message to get through. But we have to continue in faith. When parents are willing to demonstrate faith, then their influence is unforgettable. Long before Moses lived as “seeing Him who is invisible,” he saw his parents demonstrate that way of living. When you see the invisible, you see a God who is mighty, powerful, holy. This God is big enough for every moment in life, including the wilderness moments of life.

Confession: I see the invisible by faith. I receive grace to pass it on to my generation

December 14

Joel; Revelation 4

Highest form of worship

Genesis 22:5

And Abraham said unto his young men, Abide ye here with the ass; and I and the lad will go yonder and worship, and come again to you.

"And I and the lad will go yonder and worship". Abraham was going to offer his son Isaac as a sacrifice, just as God commanded (Genesis 22:2-3). Obedience is the highest form of worship. This selfless act of service is the ultimate act of worship. Jesus also demonstrated this act of worship when he said in Luke 22:42, "...Not as I, but as You Will". Right here, Jesus was worshipping His Father by submitting Himself and Obeying the will of the Father. If we love God, we will obey him in all things. Jesus said that the greatest commandment was to love God and love others (Matthew 22:35–40). We can sing all the songs we want, but if we aren't able to follow these two commandments, we are missing the point of obedience as an act of worship.

Confession: Lord, I will obey you in all things.

December 15

Amos 1-3; Revelation 5

They shall flee and perish

Psalm 9:2-3
I will be glad and rejoice in thee: I will sing praise to thy name, O thou most High. When mine enemies are turned back, they shall fall and perish at thy presence.

When we're troubled and ready to run, God is perfectly calm. When we're ready to retreat, He prepares a table for us. Why? Because no matter how out of control we feel, God is still in control. When we spend time praising the King of kings, our enemies will turn back. Be it the enemy of sickness and diseases, depression,or problems of any kind. I read the story of a sister, who was sick for a long time and was not responding to treatment. She had a dream where she saw that her praise basket was empty; she then decided to give God sacrificial praise for two hours every day, using her little strength, she gave God high praise. As she did this, all the symptoms gradually disappeared, and she was completely healed. Let your life be filled with praise and see the enemies turning back because God inhabits our praises.

Confession: I receive grace to fill up my praise basket.

December 16

Amos 4-6; Revelation 6

Rooted and built up

Colossians 2:6-7
As ye have therefore received Christ Jesus the Lord, so walk ye in him: Rooted and built up in him, and stablished in the faith, as ye have been taught, abounding therein with thanksgiving.

The strong roots of the tree are the foundation that enables the tree to grow tall and strong. The roots provide the foundation for the tree to grow and provide the necessary nutrients through the soil that the tree needs to grow and eventually produce fruit. Just like a tree, we are called to develop and produce for God's glory. Rooting yourself to Jesus means establishing a strong faith and reliance on Jesus so that you will not fall or be tossed around during trials. How then can your faith be rooted in God? Jesus said in Luke 6:47-49 that he who comes to him listens to his teaching and then follows it is like a person building a house, who digs deep and lays the foundation on solid rock. As Christians, when we are rooted in the word of God and practice it daily, we are digging strong roots.

Confession: Help me, Lord, to be rooted and built up in you.

December 17

Amos 7-9; Revelation 7

Water in the wilderness

Isaiah 43:19
Behold, I will do a new thing; now it shall spring forth; shall ye not know it? I will even make a way in the wilderness, and rivers in the desert.

Thank God that He can make a way when no way naturally exists. He did that for the people of Israel when he made a way through the Red Sea. The period of difficulty is not forever, and we should not be discouraged in the middle of the waters thinking that that is our lot in life for all time. No, Israel had to walk through the waters, but they kept walking. They kept progressing forward. And when the mighty waters rise in your life, you too will get through because God is the one who gets you through. In verse 18 of the above text, God instructs us to forget the former things and not dwell on the past because He wants to do something new and amazing for us. God is faithful, and he is interested in our lives. Our part is to trust God and patiently wait for him.

Confession: Thank you, Lord, for the new things you are doing in my life.

December 18

Obadiah; Revelation 8

He will complete it

Philippians 1:6
Being confident of this very thing, that he which hath begun a good work in you will perform it until the day of Jesus Christ.

Paul knew that when God begins a good work in a newborn believer, He will most certainly bring it to completion, which is why he declared, "For I am confident of this very thing, only God can carry out the work of justification in the life of a believer". Only He can bring His work to its conclusion when we receive our glorified bodies. Only He can continue the ongoing work of sanctification that brings a baby Christian to spiritual maturity. God is the Author and Finisher of the good work He started in us so that we all reach spiritual maturity. We were not in a position to do anything to be justified or glorified in God's eyes, nor are we in a position to carry out the progressive work of sanctification, but as we behold Christ through his word, we are changed from glory to glory.

Confession: Thank you, Lord, I am confident that you can complete your good work in me.

December 19

Jonah; Revelation 9

Pursue peace

Psalm 34:14
Depart from evil, and do good; seek peace, and pursue it.

The word "peace" refers to a state of harmony and tranquillity—both in our lives and relationships. God wants us to be aggressive pursuers of peace in all our relationships. No Christian should allow conflict to fester unresolved in their life. Just as we cannot love God without loving others, we cannot pursue holiness without pursuing peace with all men. We seek peace by aggressively maintaining peace within regardless of our problems in life. If we are peaceful within, we will be able to extend it to other people in our relationships. Many people react negatively to people and issues because they have so many things unresolved in their lives. When there is no peace within, little things can get us aggravated. God wants us to pursue peace with our friends and neighbours. We need to ask God for wisdom.

Confession: Lord, I receive wisdom and grace to pursue peace with all men.

December 20

Micah 1-3; Revelation 10

Be content

Hebrews 13:5
Let your conversation be without covetousness; and be content with such things as ye have: for he hath said, I will never leave thee, nor forsake thee.

Contentment is one of the unnamed cousins of the fruit of the Spirit, for it has conquered the evil lust of covetousness which can be identified in many ungodly behaviours… like the lusts of the world, the lusts of the flesh, and the pride of life. Contentment is the product of a God-given peace that calms a troubled spirit and brings peace to a striving soul. Why should we be content with what we have? Well, godliness with contentment is great gain, while a discontented soul breeds murmuring against God, as was seen in Israel's wilderness walk. Grumbling is a poisonous root of unbelief that demonstrates a lack of faith in the Lord our God. God, in His grace, has given us many precious blessings and has promised never to leave us nor forsake us, no matter how fiercely the bitter wind of trial may be.

Confession: Thank you, Lord, I am content with what I have now.

December 21

Micah 4-5; Revelation 11

But with God

Matthew 19:26

But Jesus beheld them, and said unto them, With men this is impossible; but with God all things are possible.

The rich young ruler was zealous in keeping the commandments, and he was righteous in all his ways, as man counts goodness. He may not have murdered or stolen anything. He may have honored his parents and shown great generosity to them. But when Jesus challenged him to sell all he had and give the proceeds to the poor. His love for money made him go away with a sorrowful heart, for he had many great possessions. He loved his wealth more than he loved the Lord. Jesus then commented that It is easier for a camel to go through the eye of a needle than for a rich man to enter into the kingdom of God. The disciples then asked, "Who then can be saved?" Jesus then replied, “with men, this is impossible, but with God, all things are possible”. Nothing we can do, earn or give can purchase salvation. Salvation is a gift of God's grace to us.

Confession: Lord, I believe that with you, all things are possible.

December 22

Micah 6-7; Revelation 12

Persistence breaks resistance

Daniel 10:13
But the prince of the kingdom of Persia withstood me one and twenty days: but, lo, Michael, one of the chief princes, came to help me; and I remained there with the kings of Persia.

Daniel has been heard from the first day already. But the prince of the kingdom of Persia withstood the angel for twenty-one days. This means that for 3 weeks, a mighty but invisible battle was fought between the angel of light and the prince of darkness. But Daniel persisted in prayer until he got the answer. If Daniel was not strong in faith, he might have concluded from the delay that there is no God in heaven and that prayer is a waste of time. We can rest assured that our prayers are heard, just like Daniel's. But sometimes, there may be a delay from the kingdom of darkness. Our response is to continue in prayers and resist the devil, and he will flee. At this time, we can trust the Holy Spirit to give us insight, for he knows all things.

Confession: Lord, I receive grace to be persistent in prayer.

December 23

Nahum; Revelation 13

You are light

Matthew 5:14
Ye are the light of the world. A city that is set on an hill cannot be hid.

Christ entrusted us with the privileged position of being His ambassadors on earth. He instructed us to "let your light so shine before men, that the world may see your good works, and glorify your Father Who is in heaven". As children of God who are born of the Spirit and washed in His blood, we have now become 'light in the Lord'. As the body of Christ, we are directed to shine the light of Christ into the world with our godly conduct so that throughout our Christian life, we may walk worthy of our calling as 'children of the light'. All that we do and all that we are should reflect the glory of the Lord Jesus for a particular purpose so that our heavenly Father may be glorified through our lives. We should be like the moon reflecting the glorious light of the sun, diverting attention away from ourselves onto the lovely person of the Lord Jesus.

Confession: Father, let all I do reflect the glory of our Lord Jesus Christ.

December 24

Habakkuk; Revelation 14

Confess your faults

James 5:16
Confess your faults one to another, and pray one for another, that ye may be healed. The effectual fervent prayer of a righteous man availeth much.

This call to confession is not a summon to the confessional box where a 'priest' becomes a middleman between us and God - for there is one God, and one mediator between God and mankind, the man Christ Jesus. and He alone is the one to Whom we confess our sins. Nor is this a call to expose our secret sins to the whole wide world - we are to confess our sins to God - and He is faithful and just to forgive us our sins and to cleanse us from all unrighteousness. When we have wronged another person we are called to go to them quickly and admit our sin and seek their forgiveness - for this is the will of God for us. We are also called to willingly pray for each other and lift up those, who may have wronged us, to the Lord in prayer.

Confession: Help me Lord, to forgive and pray for those who wronged me.

December 25

Zephaniah; Revelation 15

Owe no man

Romans 13:8

Owe no man any thing, but to love one another: for he that loveth another hath fulfilled the law.

There are certain principles that a spiritual believer is encouraged to put into action. Of all God's divine attributes, the one we are commanded to engage in and develop is love which seems to be both the guiding principle and pinnacle of the Christian life – for God is love. Love is not only a guiding principle but is a crucial part of the moral commands given to Israel. Jesus condensed the entire Mosaic Law into one simple instruction – you shall love the Lord your God with all your heartand your neighbour as yourself. Paul not only took pains to explain that the Law could not save us, but identified it as a simple tool, usedby God, to identify our need for a Saviour, and thus bring fallen man to faith in Christ – our 'sin-substitute'. He also taught that love is the fulfillment of the law and that we are to owe nothing to anyone – except to love one another, for he who loves his neighbour has fulfilled the law.

Confession: Lord, multiply Your everlasting love for others within my heart in Jesus name.

December 26

Haggai; Revelation 16

Warn the wicked

Exodus 33:9

Nevertheless, if thou warn the wicked of his way to turn from it; if he do not turn from his way, he shall die in his iniquity; but thou hast delivered thy soul.

God--in mercy--does not leave His people without the warning of a watchman. He brings the sword of discipline, but it isn't His will that the people perish. God has no pleasure in the death of the wicked, but that the wicked turn from his way and live. He is merciful and permits that a watchman is raised to give His people a warning. This is a fundamental spiritual principle that relates to us who are given the watchman's call. God does not send angelic beings from heaven to be the 'watchmen' to His people. Instead, He has chosen to take fallen, sinful people, redeem them, make them His spokesmen and spokeswomen, and leave them among the people from whom they were drawn. As Christians, God has called us to be His spokesperson--His "watchman" to our family, neighborhood, and workplace.

Confession: Help me, Lord, to do the work of a watchman by warning the wicked.

December 27

Zechariah 1-3; Revelation 17

Because they trust in Him

Psalm 37:39-40

But the salvation of the righteous is of the Lord: he is their strength in the time of trouble.

And the Lord shall help them, and deliver them: he shall deliver them from the wicked, and save them, because they trust in him.

It is straightforward to sing and declare God as our stronghold in good times; it is quite another to willingly prove that He is our stronghold when the storms of life are raging. Our faith and our character are proven in times of trial. God is our stronghold, the One who helps, rescues, and saves the righteous. God saves the righteous because they take refuge in Him. He is their stronghold; He is their confidence and hope. They will not turn to worldly wisdom or methods. They will not depend on the forces of the world or the spiritual powers of this present age. Their confidence is not in their stuff, power, or themselves, but in God. He will see them through whatever trials or tribulations they may be going through.

Confession: My confidence is in you Lord; you are my helper.

December 28

Zechariah 4-6; Revelation 18

The keys of the kingdom

Matthew 16:19
And I will give unto thee the keys of the kingdom of heaven: and whatsoever thou shalt bind on earth shall be bound in heaven: and whatsoever thou shalt loose on earth shall be loosed in heaven.

What's a key? A key is a mechanism or device which opens something. If you have the key to something you have the authority to open it up. The preaching of the Word of God represents the keys of the kingdom. It is through the preaching of the Word that men come into a right relationship with God. The key to the kingdom is the offer of the gospel. Whenever you offer the gospel to another person, you open the door of heaven to them. What happens if people go through that door? They are saved. They are born again. They become children of God, and you have opened the door for them. God has given us, the church, the keys of the kingdom, and He is watching us day and night to see what we are doing with what he has given us.

Confession: Help me, Lord, to use the keys you have given me.

December 29

Zecharia 7-11; Revelation 19-20

The path of the just

Proverbs 4:18
But the path of the just is as the shining light, that shineth more and more unto the perfect day.

The brightness of the light is in different degrees. There are higher levels of brightness. The light represents the radiance of God's glory from our lives. We all walk in varying levels of glory, and it only gets brighter and brighter. You might have experienced God to some degree. But there are higher levels of glory that lie ahead of you. As you maintain an intimate relationship with the Holy Spirit, He will bring you to higher glory. There are things in your Christian life that you understand better now, and there are things that may not be clear to you now. But you will understand better as you grow in the Lord. There may be some bad habits you are still struggling with as a Christian. The strength you need to overcome those habits comes from your intimate relationship with the Holy Spirit. He is our helper. He brightens our parts as we deepen our fellowship with him.

Confession: Thank you, Lord, my path shines brighter and brighter.

December 30

Zechariah 12-14; Revelation 21

Bless the Lord oh my soul

Psalm 103:2-4

Bless the Lord, O my soul, and forget not all his benefits: Who forgiveth all thine iniquities; who healeth all thy diseases; Who redeemeth thy life from destruction; who crowneth thee with lovingkindness and tender mercies;

To bless the Lord means to delight in Him with our spirit, soul, and body. To bless the Lord means to express our love for Him with a grateful heart that is rooted in a humble reverence and only desires that He be glorified. Human beings are forgetful creatures, and the Bible is replete with warnings to "forget not." We are to remember all his benefits. He forgives us all our iniquities; He heals all our diseases; he redeems our life from destruction and crowns us with His loving-kindness. But to bless the Lord with all that is within us calls for obedience and a total commitment to live as unto the Lord with our inner heart, soul, mind, and strength. We needto be determined to live godly in Christ Jesus.

Confession: I will bless the lord; I will not forget all his benefits.

December 31

Malachi; Revelation 22

Spiritual hunger

Matthew 5:6
Blessed are they which do hunger and thirst after righteousness: for they shall be filled.

"Blessed are those who hunger and thirst for righteousness…." Righteousness is an attribute of God. It is doing right. Righteousness should be our attribute as well, but Romans 3:10 says, "There is none righteous, no, not one." The good news is that on the cross, Jesus took all our sins, and He credited or gave to us, His righteousness (2 Cor. 5:21). We have positional righteousness because we are in Christ Jesus. But we practice righteousness as children of God. Righteousness is both positional and personal. We can live righteously like Jesus while he was on earth, He went about doing good, or we can choose to live like the world. Jesus alone can satisfy the longing hearts that thirst after righteousness. The Bible says, "Seek first the kingdom of God and His righteousness, and all these things shall be added to you" (Mt. 6:33).

Confession: I shall be filled as I hunger and thirst after righteousness.

OTHER BOOKS FROM THE AUTHOR

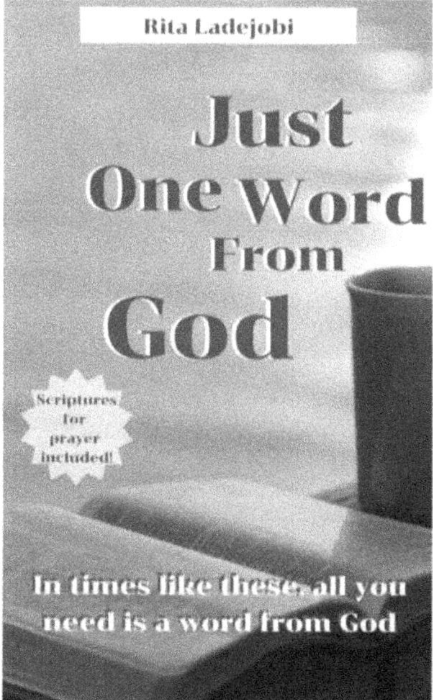

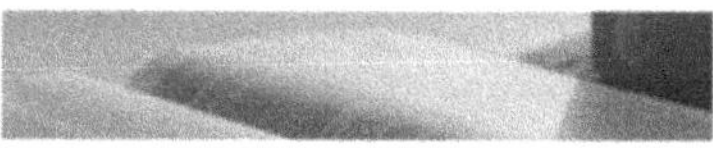

Just one word from God is a manual for every believer, both young Christinas as well as old ones who may be going through one challenge or the other in their Christian journey and desire to know how to come out of such challenges.

The author is down to earth with practical life application to issues and personal practical examples. The book provides biblical solutions to real present day life challenges of believers and where to find what God says concerning such issues in the Bible. It is a manual to be by your side as a believer so as to constantly make reference to it as the need arises because it is simple, clear, practical and specific to the issues of life. It is a must read for the Child of God who wants to occupy his ordained place in Christ.
- Pst. Chike Aku, Winners Chapel.

- JUST ONE WORD FROM GOD : AMAZON.COM
- TRANSLATED AND TRANSFORMED FREE E-BOOK : RITALADEJOBI.WORDPRESS.COM

www.ingramcontent.com/pod-product-compliance
Lightning Source LLC
LaVergne TN
LVHW010537160826
845677LV00013B/2899